SERVE & SAVOR WINE LIKE A PRO!

The Sommelier's Guide to Wine is an insider's tour of the making, tasting, and serving of wine. Jam-packed with full-color photographs, luscious wine labels, detailed maps, and beautiful illustrations, it reveals all of wine's secrets simply and step by step. From grape types, wine making methods, and areas of production to buying, ordering, and enjoying this most perfect of potables, *The Sommelier's Guide* is wine laid bare. It is a portable classroom in which diners and wine waiters learn all the œnology essentials for serving and savoring wine.

Wondering what to pair with a sumptuous seafood dinner? Hung up on how to handle a broken cork? Stumped on serving a sip tableside? Lost in a wine label? As a master educator at the renowned Culinary Institute of America, Brian H. Smith knows just how to allay your wine worries. He teaches you everything you need to know to get wine from menu to table—invaluable information for diners and waiters alike. *The Sommelier's Guide* is a book like no other—it's an indispensably helpful, no-holds-barred handbook for understanding, assessing, and appreciating wine like a pro.

ABOUT THE AUTHOR

Born in London, Brian H. Smith was educated and worked in the wine trade there before moving to the United States. Smith has taught and lectured extensively in educational programs, seminars, and conferences in the United States and abroad, and for the past 15 years has been one of the leading wine educators at the famed Culinary Institute of America. He is co-author of *Exploring Wine: The Culinary Institute of America's Complete Guide to Wines of the World (2001)*. He lives in Kingston, New York.

THE
SOMMELIER'S
GUIDE
TO WINE

*A Primer for
Selecting, Serving,
& Savoring Wine*

BRIAN H. SMITH

BLACK DOG
& LEVENTHAL
PUBLISHERS
NEW YORK

Published by

Black Dog & Leventhal Publishers
151 West 19th Street
New York, NY 10011

Distributed by

Workman Publishing Company
708 Broadway
New York, NY 10003

Manufactured in China

Text by Brian H. Smith

Cover and interior illustrations copyright © 2003 by Diane Bigda

Maps by Sheila Hart

Photographs by Brian H. Smith, except for the following: pages 12, 13, and 65 courtesy of K. Stangeby, Pebble Ridge Vineyards and Wine Estates; pages 64, 102, 103, 197, 202 courtesy of Burgundy Wine Council; page 105, courtesy of Fréderic Hadengue, CIVC; page 148, Peter Adams/Getty Images; page 150, 165, Leigh Beisch/Foodpix; page 151, 185, Benjamin F. Fink Jr./Foodpix; page 156, Eric Tucker/Stone; page 157, Susan C. Bourgoin/Foodpix; page 159, Anthony-Masterson/Foodpix; page 166, Steve Mason/Getty Images; page 168, Simon Watson/Foodpix; page 170, Gentl & Hyers/Foodpix; page 178, Mark Thomas/Foodpix; page 179, James Baigrie/Foodpix; page 182, Richard Jung/Foodpix; page 183, Robin MacDougall/Foodpix; page 184, Brian Hagiwara/Foodpix; page 186, Dennis Gottlieb/Foodpix.

Cover and interior design by 27.12 Design, ltd.

Leather ISBN-10: 1-57912-342-2
        ISBN-13: 978-1-57912-342-0
g f e d

Hardcover ISBN-10: 1-57912-331-7
          ISBN-13: 978-1-57912-331-4
g f e d c b

Library of Congress Cataloging-in-Publication Data

Smith, Brian H.
The sommelier's guide to wine : a primer for selecting, serving & savoring wine / Brian H. Smith.
  p. cm.
Includes index.
ISBN 1-57912-331-7
1.Wine and wine making. I. Title.

TP548.S687 2003
641.2'2--dc21

ACKNOWLEDGMENTS

Firstly, I want to thank all of my friends in wine who have aided and guided me over the years and who have become a valuable source of support and camaraderie—you know who you are. In particular, my gratitude goes to my agent, Lisa Ekus, for helping to start this whole process, and to my editor, Kylie Foxx, for diligently seeing it to fruition. Most of all, my thanks and love go to my therapist, to whom this book is dedicated—I will never forget.

Introduction

*T*his manual is a basic guide to what appears to be a complicated subject. The intended reader is anyone who wants or needs to know more about wine. If you enjoy eating out, like to have friends over for dinner, must host business contacts for dinner, or work in a restaurant, then this book is for you. This guide will help you as a restaurant-goer to find your way through any wine list and to order wine with confidence. And if you are a waiter, or hoping to become one, you will find that mastering the fundamentals of wine selection and wine service will greatly augment your capabilities and job opportunities.

The information in this book has been purposely kept simple and streamlined. If you want to make wine complicated, you can. But to select wine to accompany a meal, and to serve wine effectively, you simply need to know the basics.

For the customer, this guide follows a simple premise. Everybody has his or her likes and dislikes. The information presented here will enable readers to identify the characteristics and types of wine they like and to develop a vocabulary with which to communicate their preferences.

For the waiter, or someone who will be serving wine, this manual focuses more on informal settings and practices than on formal ones. Again, if you want to, you can turn wine service into a mysterious ritual for both the waiter and the customer. I prefer not to do that. A waiter's goal is to get wine into the customer's glass in a simple, effective, but not overly familiar manner. That is the secret to an enjoyable glass of wine.

In addition to my position as a wine teacher and trainer at the Culinary Institute of America, I have worked in the wine retail business and also as an importer and distributor. I have assisted restaurants in developing their wine lists and training their staff, and have given innumerable wine tastings for consumer groups and students of the food service industry. Throughout my work, one thing has become clear—the starting point for learning is recognizing that you like something about the subject. Once you have learned to identify what it is you like about wine, then you will probably develop some curiosity as to why there are different flavors and textures in it. If you follow that curiosity, you will find that it is very easy to learn about wine and to develop your own reference points.

That is certainly how I learned about wine during my years after high school and through college and university, when I traveled back and forth to France whenever I could. I lived and worked in many places around France, and after a while realized that part of what attracted me to the country was the French people's simple but genuine fascination with enjoying meals. Wine was always served. But the French commitment to enjoying food and wine was not pompous. Often it was not informed. If you stopped the average French person in the street and said "Merlot," they wouldn't have the faintest idea what you were talking about. But they were all attuned to the pleasures that wine can bring to a meal.

In the modern world, most of us drive; some of us even enjoy driving. But you don't need to know the complex workings of the internal combustion engine and the carburetor system in order to enjoy driving. You just need to know what you like about cars and how to use them. That's how I saw the average French person approach wine.

Even if the task of "learning" wine mainly requires identifying what it is we like, that still means that there needs to be some application on our part. I strongly encourage you to read about wine. You can read this book and then stop, or you can read this and then venture on to more in-depth works. Two formative titles I read early on were *A Wine Primer,* by André Simon, and *Wine*, Hugh Johnson's first wine book. They were both wonderfully informative, but also wonderfully simple.

In addition to reading, you will need to taste and to practice tasting. This is best done in the company of friends or coworkers. When tasting is done in a group you will find that one observation from a friend will help you to focus or clarify your impression of the wine. You will also find that certain descriptive words often get repeated for particular wines, such as blackcurrant for Cabernet Sauvignon, or ripe apple for Chardonnay. You may adopt these words yourself, or you may develop your own descriptors. I have never been convinced that a banana smells the same to me as it does to you. So, if I say banana, but you think tropical fruit, there's nothing wrong with that. Or if I say leather, and you think tea, we're in the same ball-park. In other words, don't worry if somebody in the group uses a descriptive term and you didn't identify the same thing.

For a lot of people who are just beginning to taste wine, developing a vocabulary to describe what is in the glass can be a very daunting task. Indeed, many of the students I have taught say they cannot smell anything in the glass. But with time, when working in a group, most students can eventually detect and describe the aromas and flavors of wine. The box on tasting terms on page 18 should help provide you with words to express what you experience.

A common question raised by my students is whether something made from grapes can really show other smells like cherry or leather. The consensus is yes! What it suggests is that the aromas and flavors in grapes or in wine are similar in molecular structure to other smells and flavors, or that the smells and flavors of particular wines simply remind us of other fruits, vegetables, or plants.

Keep an open mind, let the wine's aromas envelop you, and, most of all, enjoy!

Chapter 1

THE
WORLD
OF
WINE

What Wine Is

Wine is the result of allowing the natural sugars in grape juice to be converted into alcohol by yeast. That process is called fermentation. The combination of grape flavor characteristics, plus different methods used in the fermentation process, provide the wine maker with several options that allow him or her to produce wines of many different types. The myriad types of wine are described in greater detail on pages 26-39. However, since grapes are the starting point for any wine maker, it helps to know something about them first.

Grapes

Grapes are either greenish-yellow in color (they are called "white" grapes) or a deep reddish-purple (called "red" grapes). The juice of white and red grapes is usually the same clear color. To make white wine, the wine maker can use white or red grapes since white wine is made using only the juice of the grapes. To make red wine, red grapes have to be used because the color of the wine comes from the skin of the grapes.

All grapes provide juice. The juice contains the sugars, as well as many of the flavoring elements that make one wine taste different from another. The skin of red grapes provides some flavor, but

also provides the color pigments, and a substance called tannin that makes some red wines feel rough and harsh in the mouth when the wine has just been made and is still young. Tannin is the same substance that makes strong tea or eggplant skin taste bitter. It also causes the mouth to dry out, leaving an astringent, or puckery, sensation.

Full-flavored red wines with high levels of tannin, such as Cabernet Sauvignon, are usually meant to be aged. As they get older, the tannins drop out of the wine as sediment, making the wine seem much smoother and mellower with age.

All grapes also contain acids in the juice. These acids end up in the wine. The level of acidity in the finished wine will have an effect on the taste of the wine and will also leave the drinker with an impression of the texture of the wine. Wines with high acidity are described as "crisp" or "clean." Wines with lower acidity seem to be "smooth" or "round."

Wine Styles

From the different steps involved in the fermentation process, and from the various characteristics of different grapes, wine makers can make several different types of wine. Any of the types of wine identified here could be made from one single grape type, or they could be made by blending together wines made from two or more different grape types. A blended wine is not necessarily a bad thing.

In fact, blending is a standard part of any wine maker's tools to produce the best wine he or she can every time. Even if a wine is labeled as one single grape variety, it is likely that the wine maker used grapes from different locations, made the wines separately, and then blended them to achieve the final desired result. It is also probable that some of the wines—especially in the case of Chardonnay, for example—were aged in wooden barrels and others were not, and that the wood-aged wines were then blended with the non-wood wines. Most producers of high quality sparkling wines make individual lots of wine from different grape types and then blend the wines together. The same is true of a number of red and white wines from different places around the world.

DRY WHITE WINE

If the wine maker uses the clear juice pressed from white or red grapes, and allows all of the grape sugars to turn to alcohol, the wine will be "dry," i.e., not sweet. Dry white wines include well-known versions such as Chardonnay and Sauvignon Blanc, with alcohol levels around 12.5 percent to 14 percent.

SEMI-SWEET WHITE WINE

If the wine maker stops the fermentation before all of the sugars have been converted to alcohol, then the wine will retain a small amount of sugar, making it taste slightly sweet, or "off-dry." Riesling and Gewürztraminer wines are often made semi-sweet or off-dry, with alcohol levels of around 11 percent or 12 percent.

PINK WINE

A wine can be made pink in one of two ways. One way is to use red grapes and allow the clear juice of the red grapes to sit in contact with the skins overnight, giving the juice a pink color. The pink juice can then be separated from the skins and made into wine. This is usually how the famous "White Zinfandel" is made. Or the wine maker can blend some red wine with white wine. Wines with brand names such as "St. Nick's Rosé," or "Poolside Blush" are usually made this way.

DRY RED WINE

Here, the wine maker uses the juice and skins of red grapes and turns all of the grape sugar into alcohol. Familiar dry red wines include Merlot and Syrah.

SPARKLING WINE

In addition to producing alcohol, the fermentation process includes the formation of carbon dioxide gas. If the wine maker can trap the gas in the wine, it will be released as bubbles in the wine after the bottle has been opened and poured into a glass. Sparkling wines can be white, pink, or red. They can also be dry or sweet. The most well-known sparkling wine is Champagne, which comes from the Champagne region in France. There are also many other sparkling wines from California and all around the world.

SWEET WINE

A sweet wine is one that contains very high levels of sugar. Such wines are also called dessert wines. The high sugar levels are achieved by leaving the grapes on the vine for a longer period of time than normal. Sugars continue to build up in the grape, and many of the grapes will even begin to dehydrate and become raisins. Some grapes are also attacked by a mold called botrytis. This mold causes the grapes to dehydrate, concentrating the sugars in a smaller quantity of juice. With such high sugar levels in the grapes, there is still plenty of sugar left in the wine even when the fermentation stops. Sweet dessert wines are often labeled "Late Harvest," or "Botrytis." The wine called "Sauternes" from Bordeaux in France is also a famous example of a dessert wine.

Sweet wines can also be made by allowing the grapes to dehydrate after they have been picked, or by leaving the grapes on the vine until the temperature gets so cold that the water content of the grapes freezes. In this case, the fruit sugar solution remains unfrozen and can be pressed out of the grapes while the ice (frozen water content) is still solid.

However sweet wines are made, they are usually more expensive because the dehydrated or frozen grapes yield much less juice.

Most sweet wines are white, but there are a few very sweet red wines, such as a wine called "Recioto della Valpolicella" from northern Italy.

FORTIFIED WINE

In some parts of the world there is a tradition of adding extra alcohol to a wine, during or after the original fermentation. If the extra alcohol is added during the fermentation, the high level of alcohol stops the fermentation, resulting in a sweet fortified wine such as "Port" from Portugal. If the alcohol is added after fermentation, the wine is usually dry, like the "Fino Sherry" of southern Spain. The final alcohol level of these wines ranges from 17 percent to 21 percent. Like sparkling wine, fortified wine is also made in many countries around the world.

How to Taste

Restaurant customers will receive better service, and are likely to find that their wine enhances whatever they are eating, if they have a working knowledge of tasting terms and know how to describe the kind of wine they are looking for.

If you are a waiter, you will find that talking about wine with your customers becomes ten times easier if you taste the wines on your restaurant's wine list. If you are of legal drinking age, ask your manager for permission to taste the existing wines on the list and volunteer to be a member of the tasting team that considers new wines for addition to the list.

There are five main considerations in tasting. They are not complicated or ritualistic, and you do not need any particular skills or gestures in order to do them. In many ways, you could apply the same ideas to a glass of orange juice or a bowl of chili.

You are simply assessing what it is in front of you that makes you like or dislike the juice or chili.

These five considerations could be applied to any food or beverage.
1. What does the wine look like?
2. What does the wine smell like?
3. What tastes, flavors, and textures are noticeable in the mouth?
4. Do you like it?
5. What can you store in your memory bank?

As a consumer, the beginning steps are to figure out what it is that you like in wine so that you can communicate that to the waiter. Do you like dry wines? Do you prefer wines with a fully ripe flavor that reminds you of juicy fruit like peaches or mangoes, or is a higher level of acidity what you are looking for, similar to biting into a Granny Smith apple or drinking unsweetened lemonade?

As a waiter, when you taste wine you should be concentrating on information that you can use to help your customer make informed decisions. From that point of view, you do not need to know how the vines grew or how the wine was made. You simply need three snapshots from looking, smelling, and tasting that will give you three or four key terms to describe the wine.

If you are just beginning to taste wine, it is usually best to start with at least two wines, but no more than four. This allows you to compare the characteristics of one wine to another. Taste white wines in one sitting and reds on another occasion: It's best not to mix and match until you become more accomplished. Finally, don't prejudge. Let your eyes, nose, and mouth tell you what the wine is like.

What Does the Wine Look Like?

With two or three glasses in front of you, pour a small tasting portion (1.5 ounces) of each wine. A good comparison to start with would be three whites: a Washington State Riesling, a New

TASTING TERMS

The following short list of terms will be useful in developing a beginning vocabulary and in understanding what other people mean when they use these words. I have grouped the vocabulary words into different categories and have listed opposites next to each other. An explanation of what these words mean and how they are used to describe wine is in the section that follows.

Typical Words for Aromas/Flavors
Assertive, Subdued, Ripe, Green, Full, Light, Fruity, Vegetable, Mineral, Woody

Typical Words for Body/Weight
Full, Big, or Robust; Light or Delicate

Typical Words for Tastes
Dry (not sweet), Sweet, Bitter, Acidic or Tart

Typical Words for Textures
Smooth, Buttery, Oily, Round, Crisp, Sharp

Zealand Sauvignon Blanc, and a California Chardonnay. Try to pour the same quantity for each wine since this makes comparison easier.

Look at the glasses in front of you and try to determine which wine appears to be darker in color. With white wines, this will mean that the wine seems more golden yellow rather than pale. With the sample wines above, the Riesling will seem pale, even greenish-yellow, whereas the Chardonnay will be more golden.

What does this tell you? It suggests that the Riesling will be a light, simple wine, whereas the Chardonnay will be stronger and more complex in flavor. The same can be true when comparing the color of red wines. A Pinot Noir will usually be more

transparent and have a bright cherry-red color, whereas a Cabernet Sauvignon is more deep and purple, even blue-black, and opaque. This tells us the Cabernet Sauvignon will be a bigger, more powerful wine. The next two steps should help you to confirm this.

What Does the Wine Smell Like?

I like to think of the smells of wine as falling into three basic groups: fruity, vegetable, and mineral. Fruity aromas are often all that are evident, but sometimes there are nuances of vegetable or mineral in addition to fruity. In the fruity range, it is a useful step to simply be able to identify the aroma as fruity. Having done that, you might then go on to determine if the fruit smell reminds you of green fruit (limes, Granny Smith apples), yellow or orange fruit (apricots, peaches, mangoes), red fruit (red apples, red plums, tomatoes, strawberries, cherries), or black fruit (dark plums, blackcurrants, black figs). In Wines by Grape Type (pages 26-39), I have listed the usual fruit associations for each of the major grape types.

In the vegetable range of smells, there are the same kinds of possibilities. You may be able to identify a sort of green vegetable smell (asparagus, green beans, grass), or red vegetables (beets), or an earthy aroma (like parsnips or mushrooms). In general, as you move from green fruit smells to dark fruit smells, and from green vegetable aromas to earthy vegetable aromas, the flavors of the wine will be correspondingly fuller and more aggressive.

The mineral range of smells are often the most difficult to identify, but they have to do with earth and rock. Some wines seem to remind us of a good handful of rich potting soil, while others have what might be described as a hard edge, something like the smell of clean pebbles pulled out of a stream. It is often speculated that there may be a relationship between these smells in the wine and the kind of soil that the vines were grown in. However, the subject of soil and its influence on wine is extremely complex and better left to other texts. For most beginners, it is not worth worrying about. I will simply say this: Vines grown in mineral rich soils (especially limestone, gravel, and slate) seem to have an increased level of acidity (when the wine is tasted) and a clean rock aspect to their aroma.

Take each glass in turn and gently sniff the wine. Don't swirl the wine in the glass at this stage: Just lift up the glass, smell, and think. Keep your thoughts simple and consider the following:

- Is there a strong, obvious aroma, or is it light and delicate? The strength or intensity of the aroma is usually related to the intensity of flavor.
- Is this smell fruity? Or mineral? Or a combination of the two? If it is fruity, the flavor of the wine will probably be straightforwardly fruity as well. Any rock or earthy smells suggest a more complex wine, with mineral aromas and flavors.
- If it is fruity, does the fruit seem very ripe (peaches, mangoes, pineapple)? Or green (like lemon or lime)? Full ripeness usually indicates a fuller-flavored wine, whereas green notes suggest a light to medium intensity of flavor.
- Is there any wood smell, indicating that the wine was aged in wooden barrels, usually oak? Wood smells in wine sometimes smell just like sawdust, other times they seem to have a sweet aroma like butterscotch. And, because barrels are usually charred on the inside, many wines aged in wood will display a smoky aroma, just like bourbon whiskey or hickory barbecue sauce. Whatever you detect, wood smells tell you the wine is more complex and has layers of flavor.

In the suggested lineup of Riesling, Sauvignon Blanc, and Chardonnay, the intensity of aroma will probably increase as you go from the Riesling to the Sauvignon Blanc to the Chardonnay. The Riesling should be delicately fruity; the Sauvignon Blanc should be more insistent but still a bit green; and the Chardonnay should seem like very ripe fruit. You may find something of the wet rock aroma in the Sauvignon Blanc, and you will almost certainly find wood smells in the Chardonnay, since most Chardonnays are aged in wooden barrels.

If you find that smells are difficult to detect in any wine, then you should try swirling the glass. This pushes air into the wine in the glass, which encourages the release of aromas. In this way, you may even find that the wine has secondary aromas in addition to the primary ones you initially discovered.

What Are the Wine's Tastes, Flavors, and Textures?

Although experienced tasters use the terms "taste" and "flavor" interchangeably (and you will), it is worth considering for a brief moment that there is a difference between them. I believe that this will help you to set out down the tasting path. In standard western thought, there are generally four *tastes* identified: sweet, sour, salty, bitter. In terms of wine, we never want to find a salty taste in wine, but the other three are all possible, individually or in combination. There are, for example, plenty of wines with both a sweet taste (from sugar left in the wine from fermentation) and a sour one (from high levels of acidity). These are primarily identified by groups of taste buds on the tongue.

By contrast, there are thousands of flavors (such as banana, apple, butterscotch) that have much more to do with aroma than taste buds. In tasting wine, it is useful to concentrate initially on identifying the tastes of the wine. Once you have done that, you might then think about identifiable flavors.

A word of caution: I have found from working with thousands of students of all ages that there is a tendency to confuse sour (acidic) and bitter. Both sour and bitter have negative connotations when we use those words in ordinary speech, and most people avoid extremes of sour and bitter in their standard diet. But many wines have small traces of bitterness, and lots of wines have elevated levels of acidity that create a sour taste. It is important to distinguish between the two.

Bitterness is sensed at the very back of the tongue and is often accompanied by a drying sensation. Eating some of the red lettuce radicchio is a good way to find out what bitterness is like.

Sourness is identified by a tingling sensation on the sides of the tongue and by the release of saliva from the glands at the top of the cheeks. In this regard, "sour" wines can have a positive side: They are literally "mouth-watering." They cleanse the palate and refresh. There is often a relationship between acidity levels and the perceived texture of the wine. Wines with high acidity feel crisp in the mouth; you may even hear them described as angular or steely. To fully comprehend this, consider the opposite: Less acidic wines seem smooth in texture. There is a roundness and softness to these wines, and the lower levels of acidity are usually accompanied by full, ripe flavor.

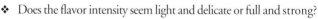

Now for the process. Take a small amount of the wine in your mouth, and start to think immediately. Consider these aspects of the wine:

- ❖ Does the flavor intensity seem light and delicate or full and strong?
- ❖ Does the wine feel heavy (like cream), medium (like whole milk), or light in the mouth (like skim milk)? This is what people mean when they say a wine is full-bodied, medium-bodied, or light-bodied.
- ❖ Is there a bitter taste (like tonic water, or the sensation from chewing an aspirin)?
- ❖ Does the wine taste sweet or sour (acidic)?
- ❖ What is the texture of the wine? Does it feel smooth, as though it has soft edges like whole milk, or is it crisp like unsweetened lemonade?
- ❖ Do you like the flavors?
- ❖ Do positive or negative flavors or textures linger in the mouth?

At first, it will be difficult to remember to consider all of these things at once, but with a small amount of practice it will become fairly easy. As with learning to dance or play tennis, you can learn the steps or the strokes fairly easily, but if you don't practice it seems like an impossible task every time. So, think about tasting (and smelling) everything you eat and drink. Smell the rind when you peel an orange; smell an apple when you eat it; smell the ketchup on your plate; smell the oyster shell when you eat the oyster. When you eat an orange or apple, think about the relationship of sweetness to sourness. Which is stronger, the sweet or the sour? Do you like that relationship? Does ketchup taste the same as its smell? Are there any flavors that you can relate to the smell of wet earth? What is the texture and taste of an oyster?

As I have said before, tasting wine is as easy or difficult as tasting anything else. Since we all eat and drink every day, there are plenty of opportunities to practice developing our senses of smell and taste and to make tasting a habit.

From experience, I would suggest that the best way to develop this habit with wine is to follow these steps:

1. When you take the wine into your mouth, keep your head slightly downward. This will keep the wine at the tip of the tongue where the majority of our sweet taste buds are located. So, the first impression should answer the question "Is the wine sweet or dry (i.e., not sweet)?" If you are doing a tasting with the Chardonnay, Sauvignon Blanc, and Riesling suggested earlier, you'll probably notice that the latter gives an impression of sweetness at the tip of the tongue.

2. As you lift your head up, let the wine sit on your tongue and think about the weight and body of the wine. Is it heavy and full like cream, or light and thin, like skim milk? Of the three wines suggested, the Riesling will seem lighter than the Chardonnay, while the Sauvignon Blanc will fall in the middle.

3. At the same time, think about the intensity of flavors. Again, the Chardonnay will appear to have stronger flavors than the Riesling, with the Sauvignon Blanc between the two.

4. Now let the wine move toward both sides of the tongue, and then push the wine up into the top part of the cheeks. Most of our acidity (sourness) taste buds are located on the rear sides

of the tongue. If you feel any tingling there, you can conclude that the wine has high acidity. This will be accompanied by a crisp texture and the release of saliva from the glands in the top of the cheeks, just as if you were biting into a lemon. The Sauvignon Blanc is the most likely to cause this sensation.

5. Spit out the wine. For this you will need a large paper cup or an old yogurt or ice cream container. It is important to spit because you will quickly numb your senses if you swallow the wine.

6. After you spit out the wine, try to conclude what flavors you noticed while the wine was in your mouth. Just as with the smell process earlier, think about whether the flavors are fruity. If so, are they full and ripe, or light and green? If you choose, you can go further with this fruit analogy. Is the fruit black, red, or green? Is it stone fruit (peaches, apricots, plums) or berries? Is it tropical? Or is there an earthy, mineral character (something like the smell of the earth after it has rained)? Or is wood the major flavor? Do you like the flavors? Is there one primary flavor that overshadows everything else, or are there layers of three or four flavors? If there are layers, do they seem balanced and harmonious? Of the three suggested wines, the Riesling will show primary fruit character, whereas the Chardonnay will offer more layers of flavor because of the fuller ripeness of the grapes and the probable wood aging.

7. Finally, think about any lasting impressions. Does the flavor fade quickly or does it linger, so that you can taste the wine for thirty seconds or even a minute after spitting it out? What is your impression of the texture? Are you left with a rich smoothness, indicating a full, ripe wine? Or is there a noticeable roughness and dryingout sensation indicating a high level of tannin, most likely with full, heavy red wines that are still young but might be suitable for aging? (For more on aging wines, refer to pages 201–204.)

Do You Like the Wine?

From all of the above you should be able to conclude whether the general experience was pleasant. In other words, does the wine have characteristics that appeal to you? Do you like the wine? Whether you like or dislike it, try to identify what facets you found pleasant or unpleasant.

One of the most frequently heard comments about wine is "I don't know anything about wine, but I know what I like." If you truly know what you like, then you do know a lot about wine. Most important, if you know what you like about wines, then you can communicate those likes to other people. Whether you are buying wine in a store or helping a customer order wine in a restaurant, the ability to communicate what you like or dislike will put you in an advantageous position.

Remembering Wines

All of the effort in tasting wine and deciding if you like it turns out to be useless if you do not commit your findings to memory. The best way to do this is to record your impressions as you taste, in writing or on tape, and that means tasting in an environment that allows you to do so. For any consumer this can be easily achieved by inviting three or four people to taste wine with you on a regular basis, and by agreeing that for the first twenty minutes you will work individually on tasting and recording your impressions. After that you can discuss the wines and what each person liked most.

For waiters, push the restaurant managers to hold regular tastings of wines on the list and work diligently and methodically to record your impressions of each wine. You should also discuss the wines with your fellow waiters, as you will find that through tasting and discussion you can build a "snapshot" of many of the wines on the list. This will enable you to present information about individual wines to any customer who expresses an interest in them.

In Wines by Grape Type, below, you will find a number of descriptive words for the aromas and flavors of many common wines. While you may not use exactly the same words, you will find it useful to build some kind of mental image of what certain wines are like in general terms. That way, when you see Merlot or Pinot Grigio, for example, on a label or wine list, you can begin to picture how they will taste.

Wines by Grape Type

In this section I've profiled wines made from the twenty most popular grape types. These profiles are necessarily general and there will always be exceptions. The most useful way to approach the information is to consider the descriptions as "catchphrases" that sum up the general type of wine made from each grape type.

The grape types are listed in alphabetical order with synonyms in brackets and pronunciation in italic type. The outline of each type will include the following information:

Usual wine style:	Is the wine dry or sweet? Is sparkling an option?
Intensity:	Is the flavor of the wine strong like espresso, medium, or light like very weak tea?
Aromas/Flavors:	What are the most common descriptors for this wine?
Acidity:	Is the acidity high like citrus, medium, or low like milk?
Texture:	Is the mouthfeel smooth, like cream, or crisp, like cranberry juice?

Tannin:	Do tannins create a high, medium, or low level of astringency?
Wood:	Is wood usually noticeable?
Foods:	What food types are best suited to this wine? (More information on why certain foods are recommended with a particular wine is found in Food & Wine on pages 177 to 188.)
Cooking styles:	What cooking methods work best with this wine?
Principal regions:	What are the principal areas of production around the world?

WINES FROM WHITE GRAPES

Chardonnay *Shar-don-ay*

Usual wine style:	Dry white
Intensity:	Medium to strong
Aromas/Flavors:	Ripe fruit, apples, melon
Acidity:	Medium
Texture:	Smooth, buttery
Tannin:	Very low; usually none
Wood:	Medium to high
Foods:	Lobster, shrimp, scallops, salmon, swordfish, halibut, bass, chicken, turkey, squash
Cooking styles:	Sauté, grill, roast
Principal regions:	Chablis and Côte de Beaune in Burgundy, (France); southern France; California; Oregon; New York; Australia; New Zealand; South Africa

Note: Chardonnay is also often used as a blending component in the production of fine sparkling wines in places like Champagne (France), North America, Italy, New Zealand, and Australia. Producers of these sparkling wines like to use Chardonnay grown in a cold climate because it provides the finished sparkling wine with a lemony, apple character.

Chenin Blanc *Shen-in Blonck*

Usual wine style:	Dry to off-dry
Intensity:	Light to medium
Aromas/Flavors:	Melon, nuts
Acidity:	High
Texture:	Crisp
Tannin:	n/a
Wood:	None to very light
Foods:	Trout, sole, chicken, sweetbreads, nut/vegetable stew
Cooking styles:	Steam, poach, sauté
Principal regions:	Loire Valley (France)

Late Harvest or Botrytis Chenin Blanc

Usual wine style:	Very sweet
Intensity:	Strong
Aromas/Flavors:	Ripe melon, orange peel, honey, toasted nuts
Acidity:	High
Texture:	Smooth, crisp finish
Tannin:	n/a
Wood:	None to very light
Foods:	Fruit- or nut-based desserts
Principal regions:	Loire Valley (France)

Gewürztraminer *Guh-wertz-tram-in-er*

Usual wine style:	Dry to off-dry
Intensity:	Strong
Aromas/Flavors:	Tropical fruits, spice
Acidity:	Low to medium
Texture:	Very smooth
Tannin:	n/a
Wood:	None to very low
Foods:	Pork, ham, veal, turkey, Indian, Chinese, Thai, strong dry cheeses

Cooking styles:	Stir fry, roast
Principal regions:	Alsace (France); Oregon; New York

Late Harvest or Botrytis Gewürztraminer

Usual wine style:	Very sweet
Intensity:	Strong
Aromas/Flavors:	Very ripe tropical fruits, spice
Acidity:	Low to medium
Texture:	Very smooth, oily
Tannin:	n/a
Wood:	None to very low
Foods:	Fruit-based desserts, strong blue cheeses
Principal regions:	Alsace (France); Oregon; New York

Moscato (Muscat) *Moss-cah-tow (Muss-cat)*

Usual wine style:	Sweet, lightly sparkling
Intensity:	Light, delicate
Aromas/Flavors:	Pears, grapes
Acidity:	High
Texture:	Smooth, delicate; crisp finish
Tannin:	n/a
Wood:	n/a
Foods:	Plain fruit, light tartlets
Principal regions:	Northern Italy; California

Pinot Blanc *Pee-no Blonck*

Usual wine style:	Dry white
Intensity:	Medium
Aromas/Flavors:	Mild apple, pear
Acidity:	Medium
Texture:	Smooth
Tannin:	n/a

Wood:	None to very little
Foods:	White fish, shrimp, scallops, chicken, turkey, vegetable quiche
Cooking styles:	Sauté, grill, bake
Principal regions:	Alsace (France); California; Oregon

Note: Pinot Blanc is also used as a blending component in the production of sparkling wines in some regions of Italy, California, and France. In these wines it is appreciated for the smooth mouthfeel it provides.

Pinot Gris *Pee-no Gree*

Usual wine style:	Dry white
Intensity:	Medium (Full, if from Alsace)
Aromas/Flavors:	Ripe fruit, apples, melon
Acidity:	Medium
Texture:	Soft, smooth
Tannin:	n/a
Wood:	None to very light
Foods:	Pasta with seafood, mildly spiced foods, grilled chicken salad, sandwiches
Cooking styles:	Sauté, grill
Principal regions:	Alsace (France); Oregon

Note: The grape called Pinot Gris is referred to as Pinot Grigio in some areas of the world, especially Italy. Wines labeled Pinot Grigio, whether from Italy or from anywhere else in the world, often show different characteristics than wines labeled Pinot Gris. See below.

Pinot Grigio *Pee-no Gree-jyo*

Usual wine style:	Dry white
Intensity:	Light
Aromas/Flavors:	Green apple, nutty
Acidity:	High

Texture:	Crisp
Tannin:	n/a
Wood:	None
Foods:	Very light seafood
Cooking styles:	Poach, sauté
Principal regions:	Northern Italy; California

Riesling *Rees-ling*

Usual wine style:	Dry to off-dry
Intensity:	Light to medium
Aromas/Flavors:	Green apple, citrus
Acidity:	Very high
Texture:	Light, crisp
Tannin:	n/a
Wood:	None
Foods:	Light seafood, crab, smoked trout, sole, flounder
Cooking styles:	Steam, poach, sauté, smoke
Principal regions:	Mosel, Rheingau, Pfalz, Rheinhessen (Germany); California; New York; Australia; New Zealand

Late Harvest or Botrytis Riesling

Usual wine style:	Very sweet
Intensity:	Medium to full
Aromas/Flavors:	Very ripe citrus, apricots
Acidity:	High
Texture:	Smooth; crisp finish
Tannin:	n/a
Wood:	None
Foods:	Serve alone as dessert, or with fruit-based desserts
Principal regions:	Mosel, Rheingau, Pfalz, Rheinhessen (Germany); California; New York; Australia; New Zealand

Sauvignon Blanc (Fumé Blanc)
So-vee-nyon Blonck (Foo-may Blonck)

Usual wine style:	Dry white
Intensity:	Medium
Aromas/Flavors:	Green fruit, grass
Acidity:	High
Texture:	Crisp
Tannin:	n/a
Wood:	Light to none
Foods:	Seafood, poultry; salads, acidic cheeses
Cooking styles:	Sauté, grill, steam
Principal regions:	Loire Valley, Bordeaux (France); California; Washington; Australia; New Zealand; Chile

Late Harvest or Botrytis Sauvignon Blanc

Usual wine style:	Very sweet
Intensity:	Strong
Aromas/Flavors:	Ripe stone fruits like peaches or apricots
Acidity:	High
Texture:	Smooth
Tannin:	n/a
Wood:	Light to none
Foods:	Fruit-based desserts
Principal regions:	Loire Valley, Bordeaux (France); California; Washington; Australia; New Zealand

Sémillon *Seh-mee-yon*

Usual wine style:	Dry white
Intensity:	Medium to full
Aromas/Flavors:	Ripe fruits, orange peel, nutty
Acidity:	Medium

Texture:	Smooth
Tannin:	Low to none
Wood:	Low to medium
Foods:	Monkfish, sea bass, fish stews, sweetbreads
Cooking styles:	Sauté, grill, stew
Principal regions:	Bordeaux (France); California; Washington; Australia

Late Harvest or Botrytis Sémillon

Usual wine style:	Very sweet
Intensity:	Full
Aromas/Flavors:	Ripe stone fruits, honey
Acidity:	High
Texture:	Very smooth, rich
Tannin:	n/a
Wood:	Not noticeable
Foods:	Nut tortes, fruit tarts
Cooking styles:	Sauté, grill, stew
Principal regions:	Bordeaux (France); California; Washington; Australia

Viognier *Vee-on-yay*

Usual wine style:	Dry white
Intensity:	Medium to full
Aromas/Flavors:	Ripe fruits, almost tropical
Acidity:	Low
Texture:	Smooth
Tannin:	n/a
Wood:	None
Foods:	Lobster, fish stews, veal, pork
Cooking styles:	Sauté, grill, stew
Principal regions:	Rhône Valley (France); California

WINES FROM RED GRAPES

Cabernet Franc *Ka-ber-nay Fronck*

Usual wine style:	Dry red
Intensity:	Medium
Aromas/Flavors:	Red berry, red plum
Acidity:	High
Texture:	Medium smooth, crisp finish
Tannin:	Low to medium
Wood:	Low to medium
Foods:	Lamb chops, lean beef, veal, liver, turkey, tuna, pizza, medium cheeses
Cooking styles:	Sauté, grill, roast
Principal regions:	Loire (France); California; New York

Rosé Cabernet Franc

Usual wine style:	Dry to off-dry
Intensity:	Light
Aromas/Flavors:	Light red berry
Acidity:	High; lower if off-dry
Texture:	Smooth, crisp finish
Tannin:	n/a
Wood:	None
Foods:	Cold cuts, ham, pork
Cooking styles:	Poach, sauté, grill, roast
Principal regions:	Loire Valley (France)

Cabernet Sauvignon *Ka-ber-nay So-vee-nyon*

Usual wine style:	Dry red
Intensity:	Full, strong
Aromas/Flavors:	Ripe dark fruit, dark berries, currants
Acidity:	High
Texture:	Smooth at first, rough finish
Tannin:	High

Wood:	High
Foods:	Beef, lamb, game, strong cheeses
Cooking styles:	Roast, stew, braise, broil
Principal regions:	Bordeaux, Loire Valley (France); California; Washington; New York; Australia; South Africa; Chile

Rosé Cabernet Sauvignon

Usual wine style:	Dry to off-dry
Intensity:	Light
Aromas/Flavors:	Red currant
Acidity:	High; lower if off-dry
Texture:	Smooth
Tannin:	n/a
Wood:	None
Foods:	Cold cuts, ham, pork
Principal regions:	Loire Valley (France); California

Gamay *Gah-may*

Usual wine style:	Dry red
Intensity:	Light
Aromas/Flavors:	Red berry
Acidity:	High
Texture:	Smooth
Tannin:	Low
Wood:	None to low
Foods:	Sandwiches, burgers, cold cuts, pizza, shrimp, scallops
Cooking styles:	Poach, sauté, grill
Principal regions:	Beaujolais (France)

Grenache *Gruh-nahsh*

Usual wine style:	Dry red
Intensity:	Medium to full
Aromas/Flavors:	Ripe, red plum
Acidity:	Low to medium
Texture:	Smooth
Tannin:	Low to medium
Wood:	Low to medium
Foods:	Turkey, duck, beef, lamb, sausage, pizza, bean stew
Cooking styles:	Grill, braise, stew, roast
Principal regions:	Rioja (Spain); Rhône (France); California; Australia

Rosé Grenache

Usual wine style:	Dry to off-dry
Intensity:	Light
Aromas/Flavors:	Light red berries
Acidity:	Low to medium
Texture:	Smooth
Tannin:	n/a
Wood:	None
Foods:	Cold cuts, ham, turkey; fish stews
Cooking styles:	Poach, grill, sauté
Principal regions:	Rhone (France), California

Merlot *Mer-low*

Usual wine style:	Dry red
Intensity:	Medium to strong
Aromas/Flavors:	Ripe fleshy fruit, plummy
Acidity:	Medium
Texture:	Soft
Tannin:	Low to medium
Wood:	Low

Foods:	Duck, turkey, beef, squash, peppers, tomatoes
Cooking styles:	Grill, sauté
Principal regions:	Pomerol and St-Emilion in Bordeaux (France); California; Washington; New York; northern Italy (lighter style)

Pinot Noir *Pee-no Nwar*

Usual wine style:	Dry red
Intensity:	Light to medium
Aromas/Flavors:	Red berries, woodsy, earthy
Acidity:	High
Texture:	Smooth, crisp finish
Tannin:	Low to medium
Wood:	Low to medium
Foods:	Salmon, tuna, shrimp, scallops, kidneys, lean beef, lamb chops
Cooking styles:	Sauté, grill
Principal regions:	Burgundy (France); California; Oregon; New York; Australia; New Zealand

Note: Pinot Noir is often used in the production of high quality sparkling wines in such places as Champagne (France), North America, New Zealand, Australia, and Italy. It is appreciated for the medium-bodied structure it brings to the wine and for some red fruit aromas and flavors.

Sangiovese *San-jyo-vasey*

Usual wine style:	Dry red
Intensity:	Medium to full
Aromas/Flavors:	Sour cherry
Acidity:	High
Texture:	Smooth, crisp finish
Tannin:	Low to medium

Wood:	Low to medium
Foods:	Turkey; ham, veal, cold cuts, sandwiches, pizza
Cooking styles:	Sauté, pan fry, grill
Principal regions:	Tuscany (Italy); California

Syrah (Shiraz) *Si-rah (Shi-raz)*

Usual wine style:	Dry red
Intensity:	Full, strong
Aromas/Flavors:	Ripe fruit, dark plum
Acidity:	Medium to high
Texture:	Smooth, rich
Tannin:	Medium to high
Wood:	Medium
Foods:	Dark meats, duck, goose, strong cheeses
Cooking styles:	Grill, roast, braise, stew
Principal regions:	Rhône (France), southern France; California; Washington; Australia; Argentina

Tempranillo *Tem-prah-nee-yo*

Usual wine style:	Dry red
Intensity:	Medium to full
Aromas/Flavors:	Ripe berry and cherry
Acidity:	Medium to high
Texture:	Smooth, crisp finish
Tannin:	Medium to high
Wood:	Medium
Foods:	Beef, venison, duck, lamb, bean or lentil stew
Cooking styles:	Grill, sauté, roast, stew
Principal regions:	Rioja and Ribera del Duero (Spain)

Zinfandel *Zin-fan-del*

Usual wine style:	Dry red
Intensity:	Medium to full
Aromas/Flavors:	Ripe dark berries
Acidity:	Medium
Texture:	Smooth
Tannin:	Medium
Wood:	Medium
Foods:	Beef, turkey, duck, strong cheeses
Cooking styles:	Grill, roast, braise, stew
Principal regions:	California

"White" Zinfandel

Usual wine style:	Dry to off-dry rosé
Intensity:	Light
Aromas/Flavors:	Light red berries
Acidity:	Low
Texture:	Smooth
Tannin:	n/a
Wood:	None
Foods:	Cold cuts, ham, turkey
Cooking styles:	Grill, sauté
Principal regions:	California

What's in a Name?

Throughout the world, there are four main methods of naming wines. Wineries use either varietal name (i.e., grape type), place name, generic name, or proprietary name.

The principal difference between wine names in Europe and wine names in the rest of the world is that European wines are often named after the place where the grapes were grown, whereas the wines of the United States and most other nations use grape variety names. For most non-European wine consumers who are used to grape variety names, the European practice of using place names to label wine is potentially confusing because there is usually no reference to grape type on the label.

However, with a small amount of effort, it is relatively easy to make the connection between a European place name and the grape type used. The table that follows the segment on Place Names (pages 37-51) will help you to translate place name into grape type.

VARIETAL NAMES

Using a varietal name for wine simply means that the name of the grape used to make the wine becomes the name of the wine. This has become the preferred method for most producers of quality (non-jug) wine and has resulted in the proliferation of the twenty grape names profiled in Wines by Grape Type (pages 20–33).

When a U.S. wine producer puts a varietal name on the label, the law stipulates that the wine must be made from at least 75 percent of the grape type indicated.

OXFORD LANDING

SOUTH EASTERN AUSTRALIA

Sauvignon Blanc

VINTAGE 1996

PLACE NAMES

When a European wine maker puts a place name on a label, he or she is indicating to the customer that the grapes were grown in a legally defined geographic area. These areas are protected by national and European law, and each area is presumed to produce wines of similar character. The best way to think of these areas is to compare them to the painted wooden Russian doll sets, where a large doll is hollowed out to house a smaller doll, which contains a still smaller one, and so on. In the geographic areas for wines, the largest area is the nation. Inside the nations there are regions; inside the regions there are districts; in the districts there are villages; and in the villages there are single vineyard sites.

The specific vocabulary for any one of these areas is an *appellation.* In Europe, the use of an appellation or place name on a label means that legally specified grape types must be used to make the wine. Well-known place names for wine include Champagne (*Sham-payne*), Burgundy (*Bur-gun-dee*), and Chablis (*Sha-blee*) in France; Chianti (*Kee-an-tee*) and Asti (*Aas-tee*) in Italy; and Rioja (*Ree-oh-hah*) in Spain. In the United States and the rest of the world, there are no regulations about which grape types must be grown in which locations.

GENERIC NAMES

For many years, several English-speaking wine producing countries used generic names to label their wines. These are place names from European countries. The three most common generic names for wine are

- Chablis, for white jug wines
- Burgundy, for red jug wines
- Champagne, for sparkling wines

Today, the United States is the only country that still uses these European place names to label wines produced in the United States. In practice, U.S. wines labeled with the names of Chablis and Burgundy are nothing like the wines actually produced in those places. Still, there are some very fine sparkling white wines produced in the United States, and some of them use the term Champagne on the label.

PROPRIETARY NAMES

All wine producing nations allow their wine producers to use a registered brand name to label their wine. This has advantages and disadvantages. For the producer, it means that they can build a loyal following of customers who recognize the name and buy the wine on a regular basis. For the waiter or consumer who may not be familiar with the brand name, it means that there is often no indication on the main label as to what the wine is, or what grape types were used. It is the job of every waiter to familiarize himself with the characteristics of any proprietary label, including the grape types used to make the wine. Consumers can easily access this information as well. Often, the information is provided on a back label. If not, it can be found by asking the wine manager in the restaurant or the manager of a wine store, by contacting the distributor, or by visiting the producer's Web site. Many proprietary labels will indicate where the grapes were grown.

Translating Place Name to Varietal Name

In the case of some of the famous wine regions around the world, it is possible to make a direct translation from a place name to a grape type. This is because the wine production laws of some nations stipulate that a specific grape must be used to make a wine if a place name appears on the label.

The following list provides a summary of the principal European place names and the grape types associated with those places. Since Austria, Germany, and Portugal most often provide a grape variety on the label, those countries are not included here. For the French section, the information is broken down into main region, subregions, and villages. This is because individual village names are often the only names to appear on French wine labels, with no other indication of region name or grape type. Where more than one grape variety is listed, the wine producers have the option of blending wines from the specified grape types.

France

BORDEAUX   *Main Grape(s) for Red Wine*
Blend of Cabernet Sauvignon, Merlot,
Cabernet Franc
Main Grape(s) for White Wine
Blend of Sauvignon Blanc, Sémillon

SUBREGION OF MÉDOC & HAUT-MÉDOC
Main Grape(s) for Red Wine
Mostly Cabernet Sauvignon, plus
Merlot & Cabernet Franc
Main Grape(s) for White Wine
n/a

VILLAGES
St-Estèphe   *Main Grape(s) for Red Wine*
Mostly Cabernet Sauvignon, plus
Merlot & Cabernet Franc
Main Grape(s) for White Wine
n/a

Paulliac   *Main Grape(s) for Red Wine*
Mostly Cabernet Sauvignon, plus
Merlot & Cabernet Franc
Main Grape(s) for White Wine
n/a

St-Julien   *Main Grape(s) for Red Wine*
Mostly Cabernet Sauvignon, plus
Merlot & Cabernet Franc
Main Grape(s) for White Wine
n/a

Margaux   *Main Grape(s) for Red Wine*
Mostly Cabernet Sauvignon, plus
Merlot & Cabernet Franc
Main Grape(s) for White Wine
n/a

Moulis   *Main Grape(s) for Red Wine*
                     Mostly Cabernet Sauvignon, plus
                     Merlot & Cabernet Franc
                   Main Grape(s) for White Wine
                     n/a

Listrac   *Main Grape(s) for Red Wine*
                     Mostly Cabernet Sauvignon, plus
                     Merlot & Cabernet Franc
                   Main Grape(s) for White Wine
                     n/a

SUBREGION OF GRAVES

                   Main Grape(s) for Red Wine
                     Mostly Cabernet Sauvignon, plus
                     Merlot & Cabernet Franc
                   Main Grape(s) for White Wine
                     Sauvignon Blanc, Sémillon

VILLAGE

Pessac-Léognan   *Main Grape(s) for Red Wine*
                     Mostly Cabernet Sauvignon, plus
                     Merlot & Cabernet Franc
                   Main Grape(s) for White Wine
                     Sauvignon Blanc, Sémillon

SUBREGION OF POMEROL

                   Main Grape(s) for Red Wine
                     Mostly Merlot, plus
                     Cabernet Sauvigon & Cabernet Franc
                   Main Grape(s) for White Wine
                     n/a

SUBREGION OF ST-EMILION

                   Main Grape(s) for Red Wine
                     Mostly Merlot, plus
                     Cabernet Sauvigon & Cabernet Franc
                   Main Grape(s) for White Wine
                     n/a

SUBREGION OF SAUTERNES

Main Grape(s) for Red Wine
n/a
Main Grape(s) for White Wine
Mostly Sémillon (sweet)

SUBREGION OF BARSAC

Main Grape(s) for Red Wine
n/a
Main Grape(s) for White Wine
Mostly Sémillon (sweet)

BURGUNDY

Main Grape(s) for Red Wine
Pinot Noir
Main Grape(s) for White Wine
Chardonnay

SUBREGION OF CHABLIS

Main Grape(s) for Red Wine
n/a
Main Grape(s) for White Wine
Chardonnay

SUBREGION OF CÔTE DE NUITS

Main Grape(s) for Red Wine
Pinot Noir
Main Grape(s) for White Wine
Chardonnay

VILLAGES

Gevrey-Chambertin

Main Grape(s) for Red Wine
Pinot Noir
Main Grape(s) for White Wine
n/a

Morey-St-Denis

Main Grape(s) for Red Wine
Pinot Noir
Main Grape(s) for White Wine
Chardonnay

Chambolle-Musigny
Main Grape(s) for Red Wine
Pinot Noir
Main Grape(s) for White Wine
Chardonnay

Vougeot
Main Grape(s) for Red Wine
Pinot Noir
Main Grape(s) for White Wine
Chardonnay

Vosne-Romanée
Main Grape(s) for Red Wine
Pinot Noir
Main Grape(s) for White Wine
n/a

Nuits-St-Georges
Main Grape(s) for Red Wine
Pinot Noir
Main Grape(s) for White Wine
Chardonnay

SUBREGION OF CÔTE DE BEAUNE

Main Grape(s) for Red Wine
Pinot Noir
Main Grape(s) for White Wine
Chardonnay

VILLAGES

Aloxe-Corton
Main Grape(s) for Red Wine
Pinot Noir
Main Grape(s) for White Wine
Chardonnay

Savigny-les-Beaune
Main Grape(s) for Red Wine
Pinot Noir
Main Grape(s) for White Wine
Chardonnay

Beaune

Main Grape(s) for Red Wine
Pinot Noir
Main Grape(s) for White Wine
Chardonnay

Pommard

Main Grape(s) for Red Wine
Pinot Noir
Main Grape(s) for White Wine
n/a

Volnay

Main Grape(s) for Red Wine
Pinot Noir
Main Grape(s) for White Wine
n/a

Meursault

Main Grape(s) for Red Wine
Pinot Noir
Main Grape(s) for White Wine
Chardonnay

Puligny-Montrachet

Main Grape(s) for Red Wine
Pinot Noir
Main Grape(s) for White Wine
Chardonnay

Chassagne-Montrachet

Main Grape(s) for Red Wine
Pinot Noir
Main Grape(s) for White Wine
Chardonnay

Santenay

Main Grape(s) for Red Wine
Pinot Noir
Main Grape(s) for White Wine
Chardonnay

SUBREGION OF CÔTE CHALONNAISE

Main Grape(s) for Red Wine
Pinot Noir
Main Grape(s) for White Wine
Chardonnay

VILLAGES

Rully   *Main Grape(s) for Red Wine*
Pinot Noir
Main Grape(s) for White Wine
Chardonnay

Mercurey *Main Grape(s) for Red Wine*
Pinot Noir
Main Grape(s) for White Wine
Chardonnay

Givry   *Main Grape(s) for Red Wine*
Pinot Noir
Main Grape(s) for White Wine
Chardonnay

Montagny *Main Grape(s) for Red Wine*
n/a
Main Grape(s) for White Wine
Chardonnay

SUBREGION OF MÂCONNAIS

Main Grape(s) for Red Wine
Pinot Noir
Main Grape(s) for White Wine
Chardonnay

VILLAGES

Mâcon-Villages *Main Grape(s) for Red Wine*
n/a
Main Grape(s) for White Wine
Chardonnay

Pouilly-Fuissé

Main Grape(s) for Red Wine
n/a
Main Grape(s) for White Wine
Chardonnay

St-Véran

Main Grape(s) for Red Wine
n/a
Main Grape(s) for White Wine
Chardonnay

BEAUJOLAIS

Main Grape(s) for Red Wine
Gamay
Main Grape(s) for White Wine
Chardonnay

VILLAGES
Brouilly

Main Grape(s) for Red Wine
Gamay
Main Grape(s) for White Wine
n/a

Chénas

Main Grape(s) for Red Wine
Gamay
Main Grape(s) for White Wine
n/a

Chiroubles

Main Grape(s) for Red Wine
Gamay
Main Grape(s) for White Wine
n/a

Côte de Brouilly

Main Grape(s) for Red Wine
Gamay
Main Grape(s) for White Wine
n/a

Fleurie

Main Grape(s) for Red Wine
Gamay
Main Grape(s) for White Wine
n/a

Juliénas   *Main Grape(s) for Red Wine*
Gamay
Main Grape(s) for White Wine
n/a

Morgon   *Main Grape(s) for Red Wine*
Gamay
Main Grape(s) for White Wine
n/a

Moulin-à-Vent   *Main Grape(s) for Red Wine*
Gamay
Main Grape(s) for White Wine
n/a

Régnié   *Main Grape(s) for Red Wine*
Gamay
Main Grape(s) for White Wine
n/a

St-Amour   *Main Grape(s) for Red Wine*
Gamay
Main Grape(s) for White Wine
n/a

NORTH RHÔNE

Main Grape(s) for Red Wine
Syrah
Main Grape(s) for White Wine
Viognier, some Marsanne, Roussanne

VILLAGES
Côte-Rôtie   *Main Grape(s) for Red Wine*
Syrah
Main Grape(s) for White Wine
n/a

Condrieu	*Main Grape(s) for Red Wine*
	n/a
	Main Grape(s) for White Wine
	Viognier

Château-Grillet	*Main Grape(s) for Red Wine*
	n/a
	Main Grape(s) for White Wine
	Viognier

St-Joseph	*Main Grape(s) for Red Wine*
	Syrah
	Main Grape(s) for White Wine
	Marsanne, Roussanne

Crozes-Hermitage	*Main Grape(s) for Red Wine*
	Syrah
	Main Grape(s) for White Wine
	Marsanne, Roussanne

Hermitage	*Main Grape(s) for Red Wine*
	Syrah
	Main Grape(s) for White Wine
	Marsanne, Roussanne

Cornas	*Main Grape(s) for Red Wine*
	Syrah
	Main Grape(s) for White Wine
	n/a

SOUTH RHÔNE

Main Grape(s) for Red Wine
Grenache, Syrah, Mourvèdre, Cinsaut
Main Grape(s) for White Wine
Grenache Blanc, Marsanne,
Roussanne, Clairette

SUBREGIONS OF CÔTES-DU-RHÔNE AND CÔTES-DU-RHÔNE-VILLAGES

Main Grape(s) for Red Wine
Grenache, Syrah, Mourvèdre, Cinsaut
Main Grape(s) for White Wine
Grenache Blanc, Marsanne,
Roussanne, Clairette

VILLAGES

Gigondas
Main Grape(s) for Red Wine
Grenache, Syrah, Mourvèdre, Cinsaut
Main Grape(s) for White Wine
n/a

Vacqueyras
Main Grape(s) for Red Wine
Grenache, Syrah, Mourvèdre, Cinsaut
Main Grape(s) for White Wine
Grenache Blanc, Marsanne,
Roussanne, Clairette

Beaumes-de-Venise
Main Grape(s) for Red Wine
Grenache, Syrah, Mourvèdre, Cinsaut
Main Grape(s) for White Wine
Muscat (sweet)

Châteauneuf-du-Pape
Main Grape(s) for Red Wine
Grenache, Syrah, Mourvèdre, Cinsaut
Main Grape(s) for White Wine
Grenache Blanc, Marsanne,
Roussanne, Clairette

Tavel
Main Grape(s) for Red Wine
Grenache, Cinsaut(rosé)
Main Grape(s) for White Wine
n/a

LOIRE VALLEY
SUBREGIONS AND VILLAGES

Muscadet
Main Grape(s) for Red Wine
n/a
Main Grape(s) for White Wine
Muscadet

Vouvray
Main Grape(s) for Red Wine
n/a
Main Grape(s) for White Wine
Chenin Blanc

Saumur
Main Grape(s) for Red Wine
Cabernet Franc, Cabernet Sauvignon
Main Grape(s) for White Wine
Chenin Blanc

Saumur-Champigny
Main Grape(s) for Red Wine
Cabernet Franc, Cabernet Sauvignon
Main Grape(s) for White Wine
n/a

Anjou
Main Grape(s) for Red Wine
Cabernet Franc, Gamay
Main Grape(s) for White Wine
Chenin Blanc

Savennières
Main Grape(s) for Red Wine
n/a
Main Grape(s) for White Wine
Chenin Blanc

Coteaux du Layon
Main Grape(s) for Red Wine
n/a
Main Grape(s) for White Wine
Chenin Blanc (sweet)

Bonnezeaux
    Main Grape(s) for Red Wine
      n/a
    Main Grape(s) for White Wine
      Chenin Blanc (sweet)

Quarts de Chaume
    Main Grape(s) for Red Wine
      n/a
    Main Grape(s) for White Wine
      Chenin Blanc (sweet)

Chinon
    Main Grape(s) for Red Wine
      Cabernet Franc, Cabernet Sauvignon
    Main Grape(s) for White Wine
      Chenin Blanc

Bourgueil
    Main Grape(s) for Red Wine
      Cabernet Franc, Cabernet Sauvignon
    Main Grape(s) for White Wine
      n/a

Pouilly-Fumé
    Main Grape(s) for Red Wine
      n/a
    Main Grape(s) for White Wine
      Sauvignon Blanc

Sancerre
    Main Grape(s) for Red Wine
      Pinot Noir
    Main Grape(s) for White Wine
      Sauvignon Blanc

CHAMPAGNE

    Pinot Noir, Pinot Meunier, Chardonnay
    (sparkling white or rosé)

Italy

PIEDMONT
VILLAGES

Barolo
Main Grape(s) for Red Wine
Nebbiolo
Main Grape(s) for White Wine
n/a

Barbaresco
Main Grape(s) for Red Wine
Nebbiolo
Main Grape(s) for White Wine
n/a

Gattinara
Main Grape(s) for Red Wine
Nebbiolo
Main Grape(s) for White Wine
n/a

Ghemme
Main Grape(s) for Red Wine
Nebbiolo
Main Grape(s) for White Wine
n/a

Asti
Main Grape(s) for Red Wine
n/a
Main Grape(s) for White Wine
Moscato (sweet)

Gavi
Main Grape(s) for Red Wine
n/a
Main Grape(s) for White Wine
Cortese

VENETO
VILLAGES

Soave
Main Grape(s) for Red Wine
n/a
Main Grape(s) for White Wine
Garganega, Trebbiano

Valpolicella   *Main Grape(s) for Red Wine*
                Molinara, Corvina, Rondinella
                Main Grape(s) for White Wine
                n/a

Bardolino   *Main Grape(s) for Red Wine*
                Molinara, Corvina, Rondinella
                Main Grape(s) for White Wine
                n/a

TUSCANY
VILLAGES
Chianti   *Main Grape(s) for Red Wine*
                Mostly Sangiovese
                Main Grape(s) for White Wine
                n/a

Carmignano   *Main Grape(s) for Red Wine*
                Sangiovese, Cabernet Sauvignon,
                Cabernet Franc
                Main Grape(s) for White Wine
                n/a

UMBRIA
VILLAGES
Torgiano   *Main Grape(s) for Red Wine*
                Mostly Sangiovese
                Main Grape(s) for White Wine
                Trebbiano, Grechetto

Orvieto   *Main Grape(s) for Red Wine*
                n/a
                Main Grape(s) for White Wine
                Mostly Trebbiano

LATIUM
VILLAGE
Frascati   *Main Grape(s) for Red Wine*
                n/a

Main Grape(s) for Red Wine
Trebbiano, Malvasia

CAMPAGNIA
VILLAGE

Taurasi   *Main Grape(s) for Red Wine*
Aglianico
Main Grape(s) for Red Wine
n/a

Spain

RIOJA   *Main Grape(s) for Red Wine*
Grenache, Tempranillo
Main Grape(s) for Red Wine
Viura

PRIORATO   *Main Grape(s) for Red Wine*
Grenache, Carignan
Main Grape(s) for White Wine
Mostly Grenache Blanc

RIBERA DE DUERO

Main Grape(s) for Red Wine
Mostly Tempranillo
Main Grape(s) for White Wine
n/a

RUEDA   *Main Grape(s) for Red Wine*
n/a
Main Grape(s) for White Wine
Verdejo

RÍAS BAIXAS   *Main Grape(s) for Red Wine*
n/a
Main Grape(s) for White Wine
Albariño

Reading the Label

Wine labels provide an abundance of useful information, though sometimes it can be hidden amongst a lot of useless odds and ends. Remember that the label is the wine's primary selling tool: It is what speaks to the customer. Be prepared, therefore, to be confronted with a lot of marketing hype along with the necessary details.

There are four principal pieces of information on a label.

They are

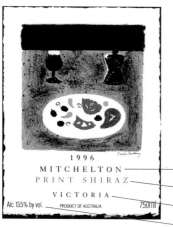

- the name of the producer
- the name of the wine
- a place name
- the alcohol content

These items may be on the main front label, or on a back label. In fact, back labels are often a very good source of valuable information about the wine and its grape type(s).

Name of the Wine

As described in What's in a Name (page 40), there are different options for wine producers when it comes to naming the wine. The majority of wines today are named as varietal wines, where the name of the grape becomes the name of the wine, as with the Gewürztraminer label on the right.

Many French and Italian wines are named after a place. (For more information, the principal place names used in different European nations are listed

in Translating Place Name into Varietal Name, pages 42-57.) Good examples of place names used as the name of the wine are Puligny-Montrachet, from Burgundy, and Chianti, from Tuscany. In both cases the place name refers to a defined area of land, and the grapes used to make the wine must, by law, be grown within the defined area.

Some U.S. wine producers still use generic names for their wines. These are mostly "jug" wines, but they still form an important part of the home market and the family restaurant market. Again, it is important to understand that wines named in this way in the United States bear no resemblance to European wines with the same name.

Lastly, there are numerous examples of proprietary names used to label wines. The label below is a typical illustration.

Name of the Producer

The name of the person or company that made the wine often occupies a very prominent position on the label. It is the producer's name, more than anything else on the label, that projects reputation. Anybody can make good or bad Chardonnay from Napa Valley or from southeastern Australia. But when a producer like Robert Mondavi or Wolf Blass puts his name on a bottle of wine, he knows that his reputation, not the reputation of Chardonnay or Napa or Australia, is at stake.

If you work with wine or taste wine over a period of a year or two, you will begin to realize that certain producers are highly respected for their commitment to quality. This is especially true if you look at articles about wine in major newspapers, or in trade magazines such as *Wine & Spirits, Wine Spectator,* and *Decanter.*

EUROPEAN LABELS

Following is a brief guide to the how the principal European nations label their wines.

AUSTRIA *Most Austrian wine labels include an indication of the grape type on the label.*

FRANCE *The famous regions of production use mostly place names to name the wines. The major exception is Alsace, which uses grape variety names as the name of the wine. Occasionally you will find a grape variety name on bottles of wine from some of the other renowned regions such as Bordeaux or Burgundy. Outside of the major regions of Bordeaux, Burgundy, Champagne, Loire, and Rhône, grape variety names are common on French wines, especially from the southern area of Languedoc.*

GERMANY *Most German wines provide a grape variety name on the label.*

ITALY *The possibilities for labeling in Italy are very diverse. The whole system can be very confusing. Wines are sometimes labeled by grape variety and sometimes by place name. Perhaps the most useful method is that of using a grape name and a place name. In that case, the format is almost always "grape name from somewhere," for example, Sangiovese (grape) di (from) Romagna (place), or Moscato (grape) d' (from) Asti (place).*

PORTUGAL *Mostly regional names or brand names are used, but grape variety names do appear sometimes. (Though most of them are unknown to the average wine consumer).*

SPAIN *Place names are still the most prevalent on Spanish wine labels, but some regions do provide a grape variety name as well.*

Place Name

All wine-producing nations share a similar approach to using place names on labels. The basic premise is that the place name identifies the area of land that the grapes came

from. There are two types of place names used: *(1)* existing political entities with defined boundaries; and *(2)* agricultural units where grape growers have identified a unique area of land with characteristics of soil and climate that make it a special place for growing grapes.

In either case, the named place can vary in size from very large to very small. For example, within the political entities, the usual choices are nation, then state, province, or *département* (in France). In the U.S. or Australia, typical wording on a label would be "Oregon Pinot Noir," or "New South Wales Chardonnay." (In the United States, county names are also used to identify place, such as Mendocino County in California, or Yamhill County in Oregon.) In Canada, province names, such as Ontario, are used; and in France, they use *départements*, such as l'Ardèche. Where grape growers have identified certain agricultural units of land as capable of growing good quality grapes, those defined areas are universally referred to as appellations. Simply stated, an appellation is a delineated, named territory, the use of whose name on a label is protected by law.

In most cases, national law or international agreement stipulate that if a place is named on a wine label, then at least 85 percent of the grapes used to make the wine must come from that place. And remember

that the place name indicates where the grapes were grown, not necessarily where the wine was made. It is perfectly legal to ship grapes from one appellation to another. While it is unusual, it is even legal to ship grapes or grape juice for wine making from one nation to another

These appellations are famous largely because wine producers have proven time and time again that they produce grapes somehow capable of making high-quality wines with characteristics unique to that place. It is this region-specific character that makes place names on labels important. For example, Pinot Noir from Willamette Valley in Oregon will taste different than Pinot Noir from Carneros in California. Even though both wines are made using Pinot Noir grapes, the fact that the grapes are grown in different places will be reflected in different flavor nuances in the wines.

Alcohol Content

Almost all wine labels indicate the alcoholic strength of the wine using a percentage figure, such as 13 percent alcohol by volume. This means that 13 percent of the volume of liquid in the bottle is alcohol. The alcohol content of most wines is around 13 percent—some alcohol contents may be as high as 14 percent, whereas others can be significantly lower. For many years, some German wine producers have bottled wines at only 8 percent or 10 percent alcohol by volume. Wines with lower alcohol content usually seem lighter in body, more delicate, and less intense; Riesling and Moscato wines are typical examples. Wines with higher alcohol content, such as Chardonnay or red Zinfandel, will usually seem more full bodied, with a noticeable hotness on the tongue and at the back of the throat.

Chapter 2

South Australia Shiraz
France • Champagne
Italy • Chianti
Portugal • Port
New Zealand Pinot Gris
Chile • Merlot

AREAS
OF
PRODUCTION

$\mathscr{T}$he first part of this book provided information on the different grape varieties and their flavor profiles. As the raw material for wine making, the grape variety has an enormous influence on the final wine in terms of flavor profile and style. But where the grapes are grown is also a major factor in determining a wine's style, taste, and flavor. The biggest player in this concept of regional variation is climate: Some areas of grape growing offer a distinctly cool climate, while other locations are much warmer. Because of the many different climatic variations from one place to another, any one variety of grape will behave differently depending on where it is grown, possibly retaining higher levels of acidity or developing riper fruit flavors. Thus, it is likely, even desirable, that a Chardonnay vine grown in New York will produce a slightly different wine from Chardonnay grown in Austria or northern Italy or southern Australia. Assuming that the wine makers have done a good job, the wines will all fit somewhere in the general flavor profile of Chardonnay, but regional variations will result in different emphases and nuances in each wine.

Climate

First of all, it helps to understand the role that climate plays in growing grapes, and how climate can affect the style and characteristics of the wine made from those grapes. During the growing season, the sun provides both light and heat for the vine. As we all remember from high school biology, the sun's light allows for photosynthesis to take place, which in turn allows for the production of food (sugar), which is then stored as energy in the vine's fruit—the grapes. As the growing season progresses, more and more sugar is stored in the grapes. This is important for the wine producer since it is the sugar that will be converted into alcohol during the fermentation process.

Pinot Noir grapes in the veraison *stage of ripening.*

If the goal is to make a wine with 10 percent alcohol or with 13 percent alcohol, the wine producer knows what level of sugar is needed in the grapes and will take measurements of the sugar level to ensure the required quantity is there.

More intense levels of heat from the sun push the ripening process forward. The ripening process is not so much about sugar production, but about the development of typical flavors in the grapes. Again, as the growing season progresses, the grapes will develop more and more of their typical flavor characteristics.

At the same time as all of this is happening, the acidity level in the grapes decreases. One of the goals of the grape grower is to monitor the progress of the grapes, especially the development of sugars and the reduction in acids, and to make a decision about when to pick the grapes. If the grapes are harvested before they are ripe, they will taste highly acidic and tart, just like an apple that is picked before it has fully developed. In turn, the wine will taste harsh and unripe.

If the grapes are left on the vine too long, the acids may decrease so much that they are hardly noticeable, and the sugars may reach very high levels. In such cases, the wine may seem overripe and very alcoholic. The general conclusion from all of this is that climate matters, and that it will have a major effect on the wine.

These ripe Zinfandel grapes are almost ready for harvesting.

For many decades now, grape growers and wine makers have referred to a system, which originated in California, of numbered climatic regions to indicate relative temperatures for grape growing. The complete system has five regions, but only Regions 1, 2, and 3 are suitable for growing grapes for wine making. Region 1 indicates a cool climate area with average daily temperatures throughout the growing season (April to October in the northern hemisphere) at less than 60°F (15.6°C). In comparison, the average daily temperature in a moderate Region 2 zone would be around 63°F (17.2°C), and in the warmer Region 3 areas it would be around 66°F (18.9°C). Those averages include the cooler days in April and October, so an average daily temperature in August is likely to be around 75°F (23.9°C) in a Region 1, and around 90°F (32.2°C) in a Region 3.

Wines made from cold climate grapes are usually higher in acidity and lower in alcohol. This is because acidity levels in the grapes can increase in periods of cooler temperatures, even overnight. So, although acidity may drop during the daytime, some of the acidity is regained at night, resulting in smaller decreases overall. Also, because of the generally cooler temperatures over the growing season, less sugar is produced so that the potential alcohol level of the wine will be lower. The higher

WHO LIKES THE SUN?

*A*part from the European nations with legal restrictions, grape growers around the world are free to plant and grow whatever grape variety they choose. However, it is generally recognized that the best wines are the result of the selection of a specific grape variety to its surroundings, especially its climate. The following are the climatic preferences of some of the major grape varieties. Some varieties show up in two lists because they are somewhat adaptable, but remember that the style of wine produced from a grape variety grown in a cool climate will be different from the same variety grown in a moderate climate.

Cool Climate White Grapes
*Albarino, Chenin Blanc, Chardonnay, Moscato,
Pinot Grigio, Riesling, Sauvignon Blanc.*

Cool Climate Red Grapes
*Barbera, Cabernet Franc, Dolcetto, Nebbiolo,
Pinot Noir, Sangiovese.*

Moderate Climate White Grapes
*Chardonnay, Gewürztraminer, Pinot Blanc,
Pinot Gris, Semillon.*

Moderate Climate Red Grapes
*Cabernet Franc, Cabernet Sauvignon,
Gamay, Merlot, Tempranillo.*

Warm Climate White Grapes
Marsanne, Roussanne, Viognier.

Warm Climate Red Grapes
Grenache, Mourvèdre, Syrah, Zinfandel.

acidity will give the wine a crisp, clean texture, similar to the feel of citrus fruit or green apples. At the same time, the fruit is less obviously ripe, showing a "greenness" or sharpness. This will also mean that the intensity of ripe fruit flavor is weaker. Examples of cool-to-cold climate wine regions are Champagne, Chablis, Burgundy (France); Piedmont (Italy); most German regions; New Zealand; Yarra Valley (Australia); Willamette Valley (Oregon); Columbia Valley (Washington State); and Carneros (California).

Wines made from hot climate grapes are usually lower in acidity and higher in alcohol. In this instance, the quicker onset of warm temperatures means a more rapid production of sugar, allowing for a higher potential alcohol in the wine. Also, the absence of dramatic cooling at night means that acid levels stay low. This combination gives the wines a rounder, softer texture, with more obviously ripe to overripe fruit flavors, and less of a salivating effect. They

This old Shiraz vine enjoys basking in the heat of the Barossa Valley floor in Australia.

seem to coat the tongue and the whole mouth with intense flavors. Examples of warm to hot climate wine regions are Rhône (France); Lodi/Woodbridge (California); Rutherford/Oakville in Napa (California); and McLaren Vale (Australia).

Apart from the general climate picture of any region, it is also useful to remember that there are variations of climate within the growing season. For example, in some places there is a significant change in temperature from day to night. Even though daytime temperatures may be quite high, the lower nighttime temperatures allow the acidity levels in the grapes to go up again, moderating the effect of the warm, daytime temperatures. In some ways, places like this have the best of both worlds: They can produce grapes and wines with ripe fruit flavors *and* with fresh lively acidity. Examples of such places are Columbia Valley in Washington State, Marlborough in New Zealand, and Paso Robles in San Luis Obispo, California.

In the following descriptions of areas of production, you

will see how climate affects what grapes are grown where, and the characteristics of the wines that are made from those grapes. The nations are presented in a sequence based on labeling methods. The countries that use primarily varietal labeling are discussed first, and the European nations, which use mainly place names, follow.

United States of America

The United States is one of the top five wine-producing nations in the world in terms of quantity produced. However, individual consumption of wine in the United States is low compared to other countries. Four states in particular produce most of the nation's wine. They are California, New York, Oregon, and Washington.

There are almost 150 named appellations in the United States, with more than half of those located in California. U.S. government agencies that regulate wine production and labels refer to the appellations as American Viticultural Areas, or AVAs.

California

Grape growing and winemaking occur throughout the length and breadth of California. The most famous areas of Napa and Sonoma lie just to the north of San Francisco. But Napa has reached saturation point in terms of the vineyard area, and Sonoma is not too far behind. There are many other grape-growing areas that have been developed over the last ten years, and some of these have the potential to challenge

The Chalone vineyards in Monterey County pioneered modern vineyard plantings south of San Francisco.

the lead position held by Napa and Sonoma.

For many years, both Napa and Sonoma tended to concentrate on the grapes used in the famous French areas of Bordeaux and Burgundy, with particular emphasis on the Chardonnay and Cabernet Sauvignon grape varieties. Today, there is much more diversity, with the cultivation of several grapes from other regions of France (such as Syrah and Viognier from France's Rhône Valley) as well as Italian varieties (like Pinot Grigio, Moscato, and Sangiovese), and Spanish varieties (like Tempranillo).

MENDOCINO COUNTY

Mendocino County is a coastal county to the north of Sonoma County. There are some relatively cool areas near the coast, but further inland the average temperatures are higher. A warmer Region 3 climate in most of the county makes this area ideal for grapes like Syrah and Grenache. There are some very good examples of Syrah wines and Rhône-type blends from the McDowell Valley appellation. A major exception to this general picture is the cool Region 1 climate of Anderson Valley, which produces very good Pinot Noir and Chardonnay wines as well as sparkling wines made from those grape types.

MONTEREY COUNTY

Monterey County is a coastal county approximately 100 miles south of San Francisco. Many of the major wineries from Napa and Sonoma have invested heavily in Monterey County over the years, but few have come to understand or master the vagaries of the cool climate, prompted mostly by an onshore flow every afternoon of cool ocean air that, at its worst, could cause the vine to shut down, impeding the ripening process. On occasion, some very good Chardonnay, Riesling, and Gewürztraminer can be produced here.

The county also includes a number of appellations, some of which serve only one winery. The most prominent examples are the Chalone appellation, where the Chalone winery pro-

The Santa Lucia highlands form an impressive backdrop to the vineyards on the Monterey Valley floor.

duces excellent Chardonnay and Pinot Noir, and the Mount Harlan appellation, where the Calera winery produces some fine examples of the same wines.

NAPA VALLEY

This famous appellation is located in Napa County to the north of San Pablo Bay. As an appellation it is fairly large, and even cumbersome, covering a variety of soil patterns and several different types of climate, from a cool Region 1 in the south around the city of Napa, to a warm Region 3 about thirty miles to the north around Calistoga. The geographical formation is a flat, humus rich river valley with two sets of hills running northwest to southeast on either side. The term Napa Valley is still widely used on many wine labels, but the Valley has also seen the development of a number of subappellations within the larger Napa Valley area. These subappellations are much more true to the unique character of an appellation, stressing similarity of climate and soil types.

The most notable subappellations of Napa are Carneros, Stag's Leap District, Oakville, Rutherford, Mt. Veeder, and Howell Mountain. The following notes provide a brief commentary about the climate of each area and the wine styles associated with those areas. Remember, however, that there are always grape growers and wine makers trying innovative and off-the-wall ideas, out of the mainstream of what everybody else is doing.

Carneros: This is a cool climate area that is influenced by the fog pulled in from the San Pablo Bay. The main grapes grown here are the cool climate varieties of Pinot Noir and Chardonnay,  used to produce those wines in their own right, but also used by several high quality sparkling wine producers in Napa.

Stag's Leap District: This hilly area on the east side of the valley provides a moderate climate and soils with fairly high rock and mineral content. The most famous wines from this subappellation are the Cabernet Sauvignon and Merlot wines, or blends of those grapes.

Oakville and Rutherford: Both the Oakville and Rutherford appellations have produced outstanding Cabernet Sauvignon wines for decades. They are probably responsible for Napa's general reputation of being a "Cab" producer. Cabernet Sauvignon wines from these two subappellations tend to be bigger—meaning fuller-bodied, with more assertive flavors—and fruitier than the Stag's Leap versions. This is because of the richer, more fertile soil, and the heat that collects on the flat valley floor, as compared to the more mineral soils and cooler, hillside temperatures of Stag's Leap.

Mount Veeder: The highest elevations in the vineyards of this subappellation can produce some excellent Chardonnay wines, while the warmer vineyard areas, lower down on the slopes, are famous for very good Cabernet Sauvignon.

Howell Mountain: As a warmer area in the northern section of Napa Valley, this subappellation has long been regarded as an excellent producer of big red wines like Cabernet Sauvignon and Zinfandel.

SAN LUIS OBISPO COUNTY

Two appellations are important in this county that lies midway between San Francisco and Los Angeles. The cool Edna Valley produces some very good Chardonnay, generally in a full-bodied style. The Paso Robles appellation has a cool climate section that makes very good Chardonnay and Pinot Noir, while the warmer climate section concentrates on Rhône-style wines such as Syrah and Grenache.

The old barn that housed the original wine making equipment at Sanford winery in Santa Barbara County.

SANTA BARBARA COUNTY

Directly to the south of San Luis Obispo, this county has two appellations—Santa Maria Valley and Santa Ynez Valley—each with a cooler section nearer the ocean and a warmer section farther inland. In both appellations, the cooler areas have a reputation for fine Chardonnay and Pinot Noir, while the warmer areas concentrate on the Rhône grape varieties.

SONOMA COUNTY

Sonoma County is a coastal county to the north of Marin county, which is just north of the Golden Gate Bridge. The general climate of Sonoma County is mixed, with a few warm pockets in the northern interior section. However, because of its coastal location, the overall climate tends to be cooler than Napa, allowing for a greater diversity of grape types in the different appellations. The most prominent appella-

tions in Sonoma County are Alexander Valley, Sonoma Coast, Russian River Valley, and Dry Creek Valley. And remember, part of the Carneros appellation is also in Sonoma County.

Alexander Valley: This is Cabernet country, but Cabernet of a particular style. It is much smoother and less tannic than the standard Californian Cab, probably because of the rich, riverbed soils in the southern end of the valley where Cabernet is most widely planted. In some sections of the valley, Chardonnay can shine, especially on the more mineral soils at the northern end.

Sonoma Coast: Although this appellation, like Napa Valley, is too large for its own good, it is important because of the concentration of quality-minded producers who sought out high elevation or coastal properties with cool climates in order to produce some very fine Chardonnay and Pinot Noir wines.

Russian River Valley: There is very high regard for the Chardonnay and Pinot Noir wines from this appellation, which have a bolder, more assertive style than the same wines from other parts of Napa or Sonoma. For the red Zinfandel lover, there are some warm sections of the valley that produce outstanding wines.

Dry Creek Valley: As a generally warmer climate, this valley concentrates on the grapes that do well in warmer temperatures, such as Zinfandel, Cabernet Sauvignon, and Syrah.

New York

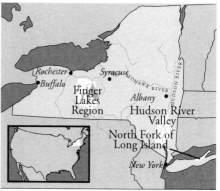

New York State has a long history of growing grapes and making wine and has recently received national and international acclaim for some of its wines. Because of the cold climate in some parts of the state, many grape growers favor hybrid grape varieties—crosses between the more delicate traditional varieties with hardier North American varieties. This means that the hybrid grape names (and therefore the names of the wines) are sometimes less well known than the standard Chardonnay and Merlot, for example. Nevertheless, some of the hybrid versions can be just as interesting as any classic varietal. The main appellations in New York are the Finger Lakes, the Hudson River Valley Region, and the North Fork of Long Island.

FINGER LAKES

The Finger Lakes region is very picturesque, with a series of green hills running north to south between the lakes. That geographic formation allows air to drain from the region, so that daytime temperatures can be warm but not unbearable. Generally, the climate falls within the Region 1 range of temperatures. The slopes of the Finger Lakes make ideal vineyard sites in some spots, and a number of producers have produced outstanding wines, when the weather cooperates. Since the general climate is cool, the area is well suited to Chardonnay and Riesling. With careful selection, some prime vineyard sites can, with enough sunshine, produce some very good Cabernet Franc and occasionally Merlot. The favored hybrid wines are Seyval, Vidal, and Vignoles, all white wines. The last two are particularly good at producing sweet versions of Late Harvest and Botrytis wines.

Vines at the very start of the growing season in the Finger Lakes region.

HUDSON RIVER VALLEY REGION

The size and volume of the Hudson River is a major influence on the region's climate, moderating temperatures by pulling warm air down the "funnel" of the river. The rolling hills that spread on either side of the river can provide some fine vineyard sites.

Hybrid vine varieties dominate here, again with Seyval, Vidal, and Vignoles the most prominent. The lone producer of all traditional grape varieties is Millbrook Vineyards, with some very good Pinot Noir, Chardonnay, and Cabernet Franc.

NORTH FORK OF LONG ISLAND

The more southerly location of this appellation places this old potato farming area solidly in a Region 2 climatic zone. With a generally warmer climate, this area is capable of producing Cabernet Sauvignon and Merlot with ripe flavors, something not so easily achieved in the other parts of the state. In addition to that success, the island also produces some very good Chardonnay and Cabernet Franc. The latter is often blended with Cabernet Sauvignon and Merlot to make a Bordeaux-style red wine.

Oregon

Located in a coastal region, the vineyards of Oregon enjoy mostly a cool marine climate, especially in the northern half of the state where most of the attention has been focused in the past. The area is attractive for those grape growers and wine makers looking for cool sites to grow Pinot Noir and Chardonnay. The principal appellation in the northern part of the state is Willamette Valley. Further south lie the other appellations of Umpqua Valley, Rogue Valley, and Applegate Valley.

WILLAMETTE VALLEY

This area has just about staked its reputation on producing world-class Pinot Noir, and most people agree that the wine producers here are doing a very good job with that varietal. The flavor profile tends to be fairly assertive, with ripe cherry characteristics rather than the standard strawberry or cranberry typical of the variety. Like all good Pinot Noirs, those from Willamette Valley have a noticeable earthy or woodsy quality, like the smell of good, fresh potting soil.

With successive vintages, the Chardonnay wines are getting progres-

Yamhill Valley Vineyards with Dundee Hills in the background.

sively better. There are also a number of producers who make very good Pinot Gris.

The more southerly appellations have not developed the same reputation as Willamette Valley and do not have the same focus on specific varietals. The Umpqua Valley produces Pinot Noir, Chardonnay, and Pinot Gris, but these wines do not have the distinctive profile of those from Willamette Valley. In Rogue Valley and Applegate Valley, the climate is warmer, favoring a broader array of grape types such as Cabernet Sauvignon and even Syrah.

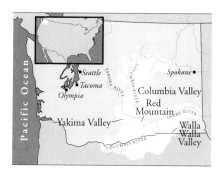

Washington

Washington is the fastest growing state in terms of wine production, with extensive areas of land that could still be planted with vineyards. The vast majority of all the current vineyards are located in the semi-desert interior of the state, where the general climatic picture is of warm days and cool nights. Because of the fluctuating climate, Washington State wines usually display very attractive, ripe flavors, with a fresh finish of clean acidity. There are three main appellations in the state: Columbia Valley, Yakima Valley, and Walla Walla Valley.

COLUMBIA VALLEY

This is a huge appellation that already has smaller appellations (Yakima Valley, Red Mountain, and Walla Walla Valley) within it and is destined to have more in the future. Because it is so large, it covers a wide range of climates and grape types, from cool climate Riesling from north-facing or high-elevation sites to warm climate Syrah from south-facing slopes. However, this broad range should not be viewed negatively: The Columbia Valley designation on the label is a very reliable one.

YAKIMA VALLEY

Located in the central southern part of the state, this much smaller appellation covers some prime south-facing slopes that receive an abundance of sunshine and favor the warmer climate grapes, especially Cabernet Sauvignon and Merlot. Those grapes make very good single varietal wines from this appellation and are also frequently blended into a Bordeaux-style wine.

RED MOUNTAIN

The Red Mountain appellation is a very small area of land at the western end of Yakima Valley. It is particularly prized for the south-facing land that slopes down to the Columbia River, allowing grapes like Cabernet Sauvignon and Merlot to reach full ripeness.

A Yakima Valley vineyard with Mt. Hood looming in the distance.

WALLA WALLA VALLEY

Tucked into the warm southeast corner of the state, this area initially received attention, and still does, for its very fine Cabernet Sauvignon wines. The repertoire has since expanded to include Merlot and Syrah from the warm sites, as well as some excellent Gewürztraminer from the cooler, higher elevations.

Australia

Over the last decades, the nation of Australia has captured a major segment of the world's wine market, and its wine industry is not content to stop there. Through a structured production and marketing plan, the goal is to place Australia in the world's top five wine-producing nations by the year 2025. To achieve this, the Australian wine industry has become masterful at making very pleasant wines with loads of ripe fruit that appeal to a broad customer base at affordable prices. It's a very simple idea:

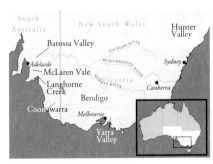

Give the people what they want at prices they can pay.

Critics of the strategy claim that the Australians are denying the importance of place. It is standard practice for large Australian wine companies to ship grapes or juice thousands of miles and to blend it with juice from other areas to make their standard wines. But, the black ink at the bottom of the page speaks volumes. Plus, if these large companies can sell enough of the widely appealing wines to pay the bills, then they can allow their wine makers to indulge in some more specific place-driven wine making.

There are three main wine-producing states in the southeastern part of the nation: South Australia, New South Wales, and Victoria. The three states constitute a "mega-appellation" called Southeastern Australia, a term that frequently shows up on many affordable bottles of Australian wine. Within each of these states are other, smaller place names used as appellations. The

Australian appellation system is still evolving, with a large number of appellation names proposed, but not yet approved. In addition to the state names, the system refers to zones, regions, and subregions. Under each state heading below, only the more famous approved names have been identified.

South Australia

The most important appellations here are Barossa Valley, Coonawarra, Langhorne Creek, McLaren Vale, and Piccadilly Valley. South Australia produces more wine than any other state, and offers a broad range of wine styles, from big, hearty Shiraz (made from the same grape as Syrah) to lean Chardonnay and Pinot Noir. In addition, there are the famous Cabernet Sauvignon wines from the Coonawarra appellation. The Cabernet wines produced here have a long-standing reputation for serious wines, on par with some of the finest Bordeaux wines or the great Cabernet wines from Napa Valley.

The cool climate of the Piccadilly Valley appellation is best suited to growing Chardonnay and Pinot Noir that are then used to make those wines, but can also be used to produce some very fine sparkling wines.

And then there are the famous Shiraz wines from the appellations of Langhorne Creek, McLaren Vale, and Barossa Valley. Several wine makers in these areas create outstanding versions of single varietal Shiraz, but there is also the practice of blending in some Cabernet wine to make the unique *Cabernet-Shiraz* that Australia has made popular all around the world.

New South Wales

The one major appellation in New South Wales is Hunter Valley. The generally warm climate of New South Wales lends itself to grape varieties such as Cabernet Sauvignon and Shiraz, which thrive in such conditions. This means that the wines from these grapes offer abundant ripe fruit character. There are also some cooler vineyard sites in the Brokenback Range of mountains that have produced some fine Chardonnays, and display signature ripe fruit flavors as well.

New South Wales is something of a specialist in the production of Semillon wines, both in

Barossa Valley vineyards in the early morning sun.

a dry style and occasionally in a sweet Late Harvest or Botrytis style. Though this is not a grape type favored much elsewhere in the world, New South Wales Semillon wines are well worth seeking out.

Victoria

The Yarra Valley vineyards of Victoria.

Victoria is the southernmost mainland state of Australia, with some very cool areas on the south coast and warmer locations in the northern interior. Several decades ago, the warmer areas were heavily planted with grape varieties that were destined to be made into copies of the famous Port and Sherry wines from Portugal and Spain, which the Australians lovingly and irreverently call "stickies." Of particular interest is the Liqueur Muscat still made by a few producers, which is intensely sweet, high in alcohol (20 percent), and tastes of dried figs and prunes.

Ironically, today the concentration is on the cooler southern areas in the state that have become a center for the production of lighter, cool climate grape varieties. This is particularly so in the Yarra Valley region where Riesling, Chardonnay, and Pinot Noir do very well. As always, Shiraz and Cabernet are also grown, especially in the warmer Bendigo region.

New Zealand

As the southernmost wine-producing nation in the southern hemisphere, New Zealand enjoys plenty of sunshine during the growing season, but its southerly latitude also contributes to fairly cool nighttime temperatures that help to keep acids high in the grapes and the wines. Because of this, New Zealand is carving out a niche for itself as producing a particular style of wine: ripe fruit flavors with lively, fresh acidity.

This was most evident when New Zealand Sauvignon Blanc took the world by storm. That wine is still a mainstay of the New Zealand industry, but is now backed up by highly credible versions of Chardonnay, Pinot Gris, Riesling, and even Pinot Noir.

The nation of New Zealand consists of a north island and a south island, both of which have wine appellations. Since the New Zealand industry is still relatively young, it is hard to suggest that the various appellations are well suited to specific grape types, but there appear to be some trends. The Sauvignon Blanc phenomenon put the appellation of Marlborough, on the northeastern tip of the south island, squarely on the map, and Sauvignon Blanc from there continues to be a favorite. Some distinctive Chardonnays have also come from Marlborough; and the

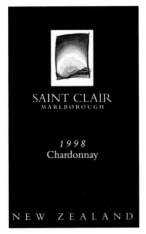

Gisborne (tucked away in the northeastern corner of the north island) appellation is getting recognized as good Chardonnay territory as well.

As a warmer area below Gisborne, Hawke's Bay has produced some very good Cabernet Sauvignon wines and Cabernet blends with Merlot. Cabernet Sauvignon from other regions has a hard time reaching full ripeness.

When New Zealand producers began to concentrate on creating some world-class Pinot Noir, the Martinborough (at the south end of the north island) appellation emerged as the preferred location, and there are now some fairly well-established Pinot Noir vineyards making wines with ripe flavors and firm structure. The suitability of the Martinborough vineyards to successful Pinot Noir appears to be related to the north-facing slopes with mineral soil content that provide for full ripening of the fruit. Some of the vineyards are still young, however, and the wines from them lack body and weight on the palate.

South Africa

Since the ending of apartheid in South Africa in 1991, the nation's wine industry has enjoyed a major renaissance. New technology has allowed the wine makers to "catch up"

with the rest of the world in terms of producing the types of wines that today's consumers crave. Like parts of Australia, many vineyard areas in South Africa used to be planted with grape varieties suitable for the production of imitation port and sherry wines. Today, after much replanting, the nation is producing world-class varietal wines, fine Bordeaux- and Rhône-style blends, and a few excellent sparklers.

Two mainstay grapes in South Africa used to be Pinotage and Chenin Blanc. Pinotage is a red grape that was created by crossing Pinot Noir and a red grape called Cinsaut from southern France. It is grown in many different regions in South Africa. Many believe that Pinotage represents an opportunity for South Africa to produce something truly unique. However, the wines made from Pinotage have never really caught on around the world, and most wine makers now seem to be concentrating on other varieties.

Chenin Blanc is a different story. The production of Chenin Blanc wines is much smaller than it used to be, but those who continue to work with it produce some fascinating wines, mostly from the Paarl and Stellenbosch areas. These are very fresh when young, with grapefruit characteristics, and can be aged into something much more mellow. South African Chenin Blancs are worth looking out for.

South Africa has expanded its repertoire beyond Pinotage and Chenin Blanc. Today, there are many other grapes in the mainstream of wine making, especially Cabernet Sauvignon, Syrah, Grenache, Merlot, Chardonnay, and Sauvignon Blanc.

For many years, South Africa has been developing a place name system, and it continues to evolve. The official structure of the place name system provides for large regions, smaller districts, and even smaller wards. A ward does not have to be located within a district, nor does a district have to be within a region. The three most commonly seen place names on labels are Paarl, Stellenbosch, and Constantia. All three of these are districts with warm climates, well suited to making fine examples of the warmer climate red grapes such as Cabernet Sauvignon and Merlot (or blends from those grapes), as well as Syrah and Grenache.

Paarl lies about fifty miles inland from Cape Town, northeast of the imposing Simonsberg rock, sandwiched between the Paarlberg Mountain and the Drakensteinberg mountain range. Within the Paarl appellation are the smaller areas Franschoek and Wellington, both producing very good Cabernet and Syrah wines. Franschoek is a fascinating enclave of French Huguenot culture, a reminder of the fact that the French protestant group was encouraged to move to South Africa to escape persecution and to start a new life in an area that was desperate for farm-hands during the early days of settlement. The French influence is clearly visible in the place names and family names of the village, and even in the

Vineyards in the Durbanville Hills of South Africa.

area's wines that tend to have a leaner, more subtle character than wines from elsewhere in South Africa.

Stellenbosch is about ten miles southwest of Paarl, nearer the port city of Cape Town. There are a few hillside vineyard areas in the foothills of the Simonsberg, just to the northeast of the town, while to the west and south the farmland flattens out as it rolls down towards the coast. Again, the red grapes dominate, with more and more Merlot being planted.

Constantia's historic claim to fame is a sweet dessert wine of the same name, but its contemporary reputation rests firmly on the shoulders of some very fine Cabernets and Bordeaux blends.

Although they are less well known, place names like those of Robertson (a district), Durbanville (a district), and Elgin (a ward) will also show up on the label if the grapes came from that area. Although Robertson is generally thought of as an inland warm climate, there is one section at the eastern end that is affected by cool ocean breezes from the south—this area shines as a Sauvignon Blanc producer.

Durbanville is nestled in the hills that rise to the northeast above Cape Town, and ocean breezes have also helped to identify certain pockets here as prime sites for Sauvignon Blanc. This picture is repeated in the southern tip of the nation, in the area

The Nederberg Estate in Paarl. called Elgin.

Chile

Geographically, Chile is a long, narrow country that stretches along the Pacific coast of South America from below Peru to the tip of the continent. Its wine areas are clustered around the center of the nation. The generally warm climate favors red grape varieties, especially Cabernet Sauvignon and Merlot. Chilean wines from these grapes are usually inexpensive and have found a niche in all the major export markets around the world. They tend to be simple but attractive wines. The export markets have also seen large quantities of Chilean Chardonnay and Sauvignon Blanc, though these wines often show warm climate characteristics of overly ripe fruit and lower acidity. There are moves under way to upgrade the quality image of Chilean wines, but such moves will not be achieved without raising the price.

The main appellations for red wines in Chile are the Maipo Valley, the Rapel Valley, and the Aconcagua Valley. For white wines, the principal areas are the Maule Valley and the Casablanca Valley.

Argentina

The Southern Hemisphere nation of Argentina includes one major warm wine-producing region called Mendoza, which produces about half of all of Argentina's wine, and almost three-quarters of all the wine produced in South America. The dominance of this region is due to the ease of farming the broad, flat fields that lie east of the Andes Mountains, sheltering the vineyards from wind and rain. In the realm of red wines, the best have been Cabernet Sauvignon, Syrah, and a little-known grape called Malbec. The Malbec grape is one of those originally planted in Bordeaux, and there is a large area where that grape was transplanted in Argentina. As a unique product in the wine world, Argentinian Malbec is worth looking out for.

On another front, some foreign investment has aided in the planting of new vineyard areas, and one interesting development has been the production of some very clean and affordable Pinot Gris.

France

For many people around the world, France means wine. This is understandable given that the French have been cultivating the vine and making wine for at least 2,000 years, and given that almost the entire nation is one huge vineyard. It is really only the northern provinces like Normandy and Brittany that are too cold to grow grapes (though they make wonderful cider from a wide variety of apples). This "national" vineyard offers a variety of climates, from very cool in Champagne in the north, to very warm in the southern part of the Rhône Valley close to the Mediterranean coast. The variety of climates also means that France produces a broad range of wine types, from sparkling and light white, to full reds and sweet fortifieds.

France is one of the top two wine-producing nations in the

world in terms of quantity (the other is Italy), and is highly regarded as a producer of very fine and very expensive wines. But it is worth looking further into the French wine scene to find that the country also produces a wide range of less well-known and more affordable wines.

Many of the less expensive wines come from less globally familiar places such as l'Ardeche or Pays d'Oc, but they are often marketed with varietal names like Chardonnay and Syrah, which make them easily recognizable by consumers all around the world. The famous and expensive French wines are more likely to come from famous places, like Champagne, Bordeaux and Burgundy. (Remember that French wines from these places are usually labeled with a place name, with no reference to grape type. This has a lot to do with the French appellation system, which is more rigid than the naming systems used outside of Europe.)

Appellation d'Origine Contrôlée

Appellation d'Origine Contrôlée is the official name of the French appellation system. Literally translated it means "Controlled Naming of Origin." In other words, it underscores the fact that most French wine makers believe that place is more important than grape type in shaping a wine's flavor profile. When a French wine maker puts a place name on a label, all of the grapes must come from that place. In addition, the wine must be made using approved grape types for that place. The specific appellation for any French wine is identified by a phrase— Appellation (Place Name) Contrôlée—that is usually situated directly beneath the actual name of the wine. So, if a wine is from Sancerre, for example, it could be labeled as follows:

Appellation Sancerre Contrôlée

or

Sancerre

Appellation Sancerre Contrôlée

Either of these labeling systems indicates that the wine meets all the legal requirements to call itself Sancerre.

The Appellation Contrôlée wines of France are considered to be the highest quality. There are other categories of French wine that fall below the Appellation Contrôlée level, such as *Vin de Pays*, which plays a large role in the export markets. This category is considered to include good but not extraordinary wines—but that does not mean they are bad! The exact origin of the grapes for wines in this category can be identified by a phrase on the label: "Vin de Pays de (Place Name)."

The most ordinary category of French wine is called *Vin de Table de France*. With no indication of grape variety and no mention of any specific place, all you know is that the wine is red or white and was made from grapes grown somewhere in France.

Within the Appellation d'Origine Contrôlée system, there is an approved list of grape types for each official appellation in France. Sometimes the list is one grape long; the longest grape list in France contains thirteen varieties. If the approved list has only one grape, wine makers have to use that grape to make the wine and must put the place name on the label. For example, if someone wants to make a white wine and put a Burgundy place name on the label, the wine must be made from Chardonnay grapes grown in a subappellation of Burgundy. If someone wants to make a red wine and put a Burgundy place name on the label, they must use Pinot Noir grapes grown in that region of Burgundy.

If the approved list of grapes has more than one grape type allowed, it is possible to use any number of those grapes in any proportion a wine maker chooses. For example, the

The phrase Appellation Châteauneuf-du-Pape Contrôlée guarantees that the wine meets all the legal requirements for that region.

approved list for red Bordeaux wines includes six red grapes. Most wine makers in Bordeaux use only three of those to make their wine, and they change the percentages of each grape type in the blend almost every year, but only with minor variations in the percentages.

In other respects, the appellation system in France is like that in any other country. There are large named areas, with smaller subsections within them. It is generally true that the smaller a wine's named place of origin, the higher its price will be. Most French wine regions have a sort of hierarchy of place, which can be described as going from a large region, to smaller districts, and then down to villages. Within the villages there are even smaller named units of land. These are the individual vineyard sites. If all of the grapes came from one single vineyard, the wine maker has the right to put the name of that vineyard on the label.

In some parts of France, many of the small vineyard sites have been classified into rankings such as *Premier Cru* and *Grand Cru*. When a title like this shows up on a label, the wine will be expensive and it should be of exceptional quality since the grapes came from a vineyard that has been recognized over centuries as capable of producing outstanding grapes.

The classic wine appellations in France are Alsace, Beaujolais, Bordeaux, Burgundy, Champagne, Loire Valley, and Rhône Valley. The other areas to be considered all lie in the broad sweep of land that curves around the southern French coast from Spain to Italy. They include Languedoc, Roussillon, and Provence, all of which produce Appellation Contrôlée wines as well as Vin de Pays wines.

Alsace

Alsace is a convenient place to start with French wines because it is the one classic French region that uses grape variety names to label their wines. The main grape varieties grown here

A typical label from Alsace, showing a grape variety name.

are Riesling, Gewürztraminer, Pinot Gris, Pinot Blanc, and Muscat. All of these are made as dry wines for the most part, though there are some sweet versions.

In the dry wine category, Riesling is something of an odd man out since it is typically made in a lean, spare style, with high acidity and lots of green fruit characteristics. The other grape varieties are usually produced as full-bodied, rich versions with lots of ripe, exotic fruit character. Gewürztraminer from Alsace is the archetypal exotic fruit wine with spicy overtones of cinnamon and nutmeg. Pinot Blanc would be the lightest in this family group, and Pinot Gris and Muscat lie somewhere in the middle.

Sweet versions of these wines are identified by one of these two phrases: *Vendange Tardive* (Late Harvest) or *Sélection de Grains Nobles* (Botrytis affected). Both types are very rich and sweet.

Beaujolais

A colorful landscape in all seasons is possibly one reason why the people of Beaujolais have a reputation as earthbound folk with a zest for life and fun. Their charm is reflected in their simple but adorable wine. Place names are used to label Beaujolais

A Beaujolais wine from Morgon, one of the ten villages permitted to use their name on the label.

wines, but don't let that intimidate you—there is an uncomplicated side to Beaujolais. There is essentially one style of wine (light, simple, fruity red) made from one grape type (Gamay). An easy way to think of Beaujolais is as the perfect red wine for those people who think they don't like red wine. In its simplest versions, it has lots of fresh, red berry character and none of the harsh roughness of wines like Cabernet Sauvignon.

There is something of a hierarchy to the different official types of Beaujolais. The basic version is labeled simply as Beaujolais. If the wine is labeled Beaujolais-Villages, that indicates that the grapes were grown in a smaller area within the large Beaujolais region. Theoretically, Beaujolais-Villages wine should be a bit more full-flavored than simple Beaujolais.

What many people consider to be the finest forms of Beaujolais wine come from ten special villages, each of which is allowed to use the particular village name on the label as the name of the wine. Those villages are Brouilly, Côte-de-Brouilly, Chénas, Chiroubles, Fleurie, Juliénas, Morgon, Moulin-à-Vent, Regnié, and St-Amour. In each case, the vineyards within these villages are blessed by south-facing slopes or mineral-rich soils that provide ripe fruit characteristics and distinct flavors in the wines.

There is also the phenomenon of Beaujolais Nouveau, the new wine of the most recent vintage that is produced very quickly after the harvest and finds its way onto store shelves and restaurant tables all around the world as early as the third Thursday in November. Beaujolais Nouveau is the epitome of light, easy-to-drink red wine.

Bordeaux

Many things have combined to make Bordeaux so famous around the world. First of all, it is a coastal region with a port city. Through the 1800s and 1900s, this meant that wine producers were able to control what was exported to other countries and ensure that Bordeaux wines received preferential treatment. Second, it was one of the first areas in France to promote its classified wines, which suggested that those wines were of superior quality. And third, its complex naming methods—the very notion of calling a wine "Château ABC"—had and continues to have immediate appeal for many consumers. (It is worth pointing out, however, that the use of the word "château"

in the name of the wine does not necessarily mean that there is a "castle," or even any building on the grounds of the estate. It is simply a naming convention that suggests that the grapes used to make the wine came from one property.)

Bordeaux is the largest appellation in France, and produces wine of all types, from dry red to rosé, sweet white and sparkling. It is most well known for its dry reds and sweet whites from famous châteaux like Château Latour and Château d'Yquem. Bordeaux is one of those places where the appellations range from the large Bordeaux region, down to smaller districts, and then down to villages. There are several hundred châteaux that fall within the large Bordeaux regional appellation, and they can be identified by the phrase "Appellation Bordeaux Contrôlée" on the label.

The main districts within Bordeaux for red wines are Graves, Haut-Médoc, Médoc, Pomerol, and St-Emilion; the main districts for dry white wines are Entre-Deux-Mers, and Graves, and for sweet white wines the main districts are Barsac and Sauternes. Wines made by châteaux located in any one of these districts can be identified by the phrase "Appellation (District Name) Contrôlée" on the label, for example, Appellation Graves Contrôlée.

Wine made at Château Saint Sulpice falls within the regional category of Appellation Bordeaux Contrôlée.

In Bordeaux, however, single vineyards or estates that produce wine under a château name cannot use that château name as an appellation. But Bordeaux does have classifications—such as *Grand Cru* and *Premier Cru*—that rank the estates. These classifications are pretty confusing, and vary from region to region, though they often use the same, or similar, terminology. (For a regional breakdown of these classifications, refer to the box on page 94.)

There are regional and district wines that are labeled with the name of the region or district where the grapes were grown. These wines are produced by large companies, called *négociants*, who purchase surplus grapes or wine from small estates and then put

REGIONAL BREAKDOWN OF BORDEAUX CLASSIFICATIONS

To keep the following numbers in perspective, bear in mind that there are thousands of châteaux in the entire Bordeaux region.

MÉDOC Since 1855, sixty châteaux in Médoc have been granted the classification *Grand Cru Classé*, and they are entitled to print that phrase on the label. Those sixty châteaux are subdivided into five groupings: *Premier Grand Cru Classé, Deuxième Grand Cru Classé, Troisième Grand Cru Classé, Quatrième Grand Cru Classé,* and *Cinqième Grand Cru Classé*.

The first grouping of five châteaux (which includes Château Haut-Brion from the Graves district) may print the phrase *Premier Grand Cru Classé* on the label. The châteaux in the other groupings use the phrase *Grand Cru Classé* on the label, but do not advertise which grouping they are in. The usual English translation for these phrases is First Growth, Second Growth, and so on. There is nothing mediocre or second class about being a Fifth Growth château. It means that the wine is among the sixty finest of Médoc.

GRAVES The Graves district has identified ten white wines and thirteen reds as *Cru Classé* wines. Some châteaux show up in both lists, with a total of sixteen estates represented.

ST-EMILION This is the only district that has a systematic review of the classification, approximately every ten years. The most recent classification was published in 1996. It has three categories: *Premier Grand Cru Classé*, class A, with two châteaux listed; *Premier Grand Cru Classé*, class B, with eleven châteaux listed; and *Grand Cru Classé*, with fifty-five châteaux listed.

SAUTERNES AND BARSAC A total of twenty-six châteaux are classified from these two sweet white wine-producing districts. The different groupings within the classification are *Premier Grand Cru Supérieur*, with only one château listed; *Premier Cru Classé*, with eleven châteaux listed; and *Deuxième Cru Classé*, with fourteen châteaux listed.

The districts of Pomerol (red wines) and Entre-Deux-Mers (dry white wines) have no classification system.

together a blend. In contrast, if a wine is made from grapes grown on the land of one single château, the wine will carry the château name on the label. In such cases, the château itself is considered to be the "producer" of the wine.

Bordeaux is planted with grapes suitable to its moderately warm climate. The three main grape varieties approved for red wine production are Cabernet Sauvignon, Merlot, and Cabernet Franc. These grapes are planted in different percentages on each estate, and every year the wine maker assesses the quality of the wine made from each grape type before deciding what proportions will be used in the blend for that year. Three other red grapes are also permitted (Malbec, Petit Verdot, and Carmenère), but they are used rarely, and even then in very small percentages.

The same blending system is used in the production of white wines, for which the two main approved grape types are Sauvignon Blanc and Sémillon. Muscadelle is used by some estates as an aromatic component in the blend for sweet white wines.

GRAVES, HAUT-MÉDOC, AND MÉDOC RED WINES

This group of three red wine-producing districts is often referred to collectively as the "Left Bank," since the vineyards lie on the left side of a large estuary called the Gironde, and the river that feeds it, called the Garonne. Also, for convenience, the two districts of Haut-Médoc and Médoc are often lumped under the shorter name of Médoc.

The distinguishing feature of Left Bank red wines is that the dominant grape in the blend is usually Cabernet Sauvignon, with Merlot and Cabernet Franc used in varying proportions to add complexity and softness to the normally hard Cabernet Sauvignon. This means that, on average, red wines from Left Bank châteaux will retain a high level of astringency, and can be aged for at least five years, often ten, before they show signs of mellowing.

Within the Graves district, there is one subappellation, made up of the villages of Pessac-Léognan. It is here that the finer estates of Graves are located. Wines from this specific subappellation will be identifiable by the phrase "Appellation Pessac-

Léognan Contrôlée" on the label. The finest château wines of Graves are ranked in a classification that dates from 1959. If a château is listed in that classification, the phrase *Grand Cru* will appear on the label. However, there are plenty of non-*Grand Cru* wines from the Graves district that offer high quality and good value.

In the Médoc area, there are six villages with subappellation status, and all of the famous châteaux of Médoc lie in one of these villages. The exact location of the château can be recognized by the phrase "Appellation (village name) Contrôlée" on the label. The six villages are St-Estephe, Pauillac, St-Julien, Margaux, Listrac, and Moulis.

The great (and expensive) wines of Médoc are classified in what is usually referred to as "the 1855 Classification." This is a list of sixty-one châteaux that are then subdivided into five groupings. The official French language for each of the groupings is *Premier Grand Cru Classé; Deuxième Grand Cru Classé; Troisième Grand Cru Classé; Quatrième Grand Cru Classé; Cinquième Grand Cru Classé*. The usual English translations are First Growth, Second Growth, and so on. (For more on these groupings, see the box on page 94.)

The five famous First Growth Wines are Château Haut-Brion, Château Lafite-Rothschild, Château Latour, Château Margaux, and Château Mouton-Rothschild. Oddly enough, Château Haut-Brion is in fact located in the Graves district.

Again, the absence of any of those fancy phrases on a Médoc wine label does not mean that the wine is of poor quality. There are plenty of high-quality Médoc wines that were not included in the original list of 1855. Some very affordable, good-quality Médoc wines carry the phrase *Cru Bourgeois* or *Cru Artisanal*. I guess we can infer from this that the First to Fifth Growths are the aristocracy of Médoc wines, and the Bourgeois and Artisanal labels represent good, honest, hard-working wines!

POMEROL AND
ST-EMILION RED WINES

In contrast to the Left Bank wines, the Right Bank wines of Pomerol and St-Emilion are usually made with Merlot as the dominant grape, with Cabernet Sauvignon and Cabernet Franc used to round out the blend. Because of the higher percentage of Merlot, Right Bank wines seem to be softer when the wines

are first made and will usually mature more quickly.

Many of the châteaux in St-Emilion are included in a classification that is updated every ten years. The most recent update occurred in 1996, when some châteaux were elevated, and some were demoted. The two tiers in this classification are *Premier Grand Cru Classé* denoting superlative wines, and *Grand Cru Classé*, indicating very good but not great wines.

The châteaux of Pomerol have never been classified.

ENTRE-DEUX-MERS AND
GRAVES DRY WHITE WINES

Although the appellation contrôlée laws list the two main grape types for white Bordeaux wines as Sauvignon Blanc and Semillon, a large number of producers of Entre-Deux-Mers wines have opted for using only the Sauvignon Blanc, which produces a very clean, crisp fruity wine with no wood aging.

In contrast, dry white Graves wines are more likely to include a percentage of the Semillon grape type, and they are more likely to have a small amount of wood aging. This makes Graves white wines more complex and full bodied than the average Entre-Deux-Mers.

As with red wines from Graves, the better white Graves wines come from the smaller subappellation of Pessac-Léognan, and the finest white Graves wines have been classified as *Grand Cru.*

BARSAC AND SAUTERNES SWEET WHITE WINES

These two districts lie to the south of the River Garonne, within the southwestern tip of the Graves district. Their geographic situation means that the arrival of botrytis in the vineyards is guaranteed almost every year. As cold night air tumbles off the northern bank of the river and hits the relatively warmer river, mists form almost every morning during late September and October, and then spread through the gently rolling vineyard landscape.

For a wine to carry the phrase "Appellation Barsac Contrôlée" or "Appellation Sauternes Contrôlée" on the label, the grapes must have been affected by the Botrytis mold that makes the grapes lose water content and allows the wine maker to produce a rich, concentrated, sweet white wine that is served in small quantities as a dessert wine.

Twenty-six châteaux in Barsac and Sauternes were classified in 1855. In that list, the great Château d'Yquem, in Sauternes, has been granted exclusive use of the title *Premier Grand Cru Supérieur*,

suggesting that it stands head and shoulders above all others. The other twenty-five châteaux fall into either *Premier Cru Classé* (First Growth) or *Deuxième Cru Classé* (Second Growth). There are several other unclassified châteaux that also produce very good dessert-style wines from these districts.

Burgundy

The Burgundy vineyards are centered on a series of broken hills that run south-southwest to north-northeast. The confluence of several smaller geological fault lines with one major fault line has resulted in a number of different exposures and soil types. The general exposure of the hills is to the east, providing plenty of early morning sun to warm the vines, but the contour lines occasionally shift around to the south providing a few prized spots with longer sunshine hours.

Burgundy fascinates wine lovers because it has been widely

praised as producing what are arguably the world's best versions of Pinot Noir and Chardonnay as single varietal wines. Those two varietals are the legally permitted grape types if a Burgundy place name is on the label. The cool climate of the region is the primary reason that Pinot Noir and Chardonnay are grown.

As in other parts of France, the large regional Burgundy (*Bourgogne* in French) appellation includes smaller district appellations and village appellations. If all of the grapes used to make the wine came from many different locations within the region, the wine will be identified as "Appellation Bourgogne Contrôlée." If the grapes used to make the wine all came from one of the smaller districts, or from vineyards within a village, the wine will be identified as "Appellation (District Name) Contrôlée," or as "Appellation (Village Name) Contrôlée."

A regional wine from Burgundy, identified as Appellation Bourgogne Contrôlée.

Burgundy also has a large number of individual vineyards that have been classified as *Premier Cru* and *Grand Cru*. The title *Premier Cru* or *Grand Cru* is based on the reputation of a particular vineyard site to consistently produce grapes of outstanding quality. It is important to remember that the title is given to the piece of land, not to the wine maker. Over the years, there have been a few promotions, but there have never been any demotions. Because of the structure of the Burgundy wine business, grapes from these special vineyards can be purchased by a number of different producers, so that, in the same vintage year, there may be more than two different versions of wine from one single vineyard.

Left: The vineyard name on this premier Cru label is Clos des Chênes, located in the village of Volnay. Right: A Grand Cru vineyard label, where Echezeaux is the name of the vineyard.

A *Premier Cru* vineyard wine will be named in the following manner: Village Name plus Vineyard Name, such as Volnay Clos des Chênes. Underneath the name of the wine the phrase "Appellation (Village Name) 1er Cru Contrôlée" will appear (*"1er"* in French is the same as "1st" in English; it's an abbreviation for *"Premier"*—"First.")

The *Grand Cru* level wines are considered to be the finest that Burgundy produces. A *Grand Cru* vineyard wine will carry the name of the vineyard as the name of the wine. Underneath the name of the wine there will be the simple phrase "Appellation Contrôlée," or "Appellation (Name of Vineyard) Contrôlée." Nowadays, most *Grand Cru* wines carry that phrase somewhere on the label, but it was not always so. When buying great Burgundy, there is a major element of having to know what you are buying, because the label will not always tell you. (Of course, the high price should give it away!)

The major districts within Burgundy are Chablis, Côte de Beaune, Côte Chalonnaise, Côte de Nuits, and Maconnais. As a useful note, the use of the word *Côte* or *Coteaux* on any French wine label indicates that the vineyards are on a slope, usually near or next to a river. Also, the addition of the word "Villages" to any district name on a French wine label indicates that the grapes came from one or more of a select number of villages within the district. This is true for the other French regions as well.

CHABLIS

This district is physically separate from the rest of Burgundy. It produces only white wines from the Chardonnay grape. The very cool climate here results in Chardonnay wines that are very different from the average Australian or Californian Chardonnay. Most Chablis wines show high acidity, a crisp, clean texture, and lean fruit character. Also a large number of Chablis wines are exposed to very little or no wood aging. Remember that in the past, various other nations adopted the word Chablis to label ordinary white wine. Currently, the United States is the only nation that continues that practice. American "Chablis" bears no resemblance to true French Chablis.

The regional wines are labeled simply "Chablis." If the wine is made from grapes from several *Premier Cru* vineyards, the wine is labeled "Chablis Premier Cru." If the grapes came from one single *Premier Cru* vineyard, the name of the single vineyard will also be on the label. There are forty *Premier Cru* vineyards in Chablis; the five most often seen are Fourchaume, Mont de Milieu, Montée de Tonnerre, Montmains, and Vaillons.

The same naming for-  mula applies to *Grand Cru* wines from Chablis. There are seven *Grand Cru* vineyards: Blanchot, Bougros, Grenouilles, Les Clos, Les Preuses, Valmur, and Vaudésir.

Premier Cru and *Grand Cru* Chablis wines show much more ripeness of fruit than ordinary Chablis, and are usually exposed to wood aging, which makes them much more complex and long-lived wines.

CÔTE DE BEAUNE

This district is most famous for its very fine white wines, even though it produces a fairly large quantity of red wine as well. There are three different district appellations that may show up on the label as the name of the wine, depending on where the grapes were grown. Those appellations are "Côte de Beaune" (mostly red wines), "Côte de Beaune Villages" (red wines only), and "Hautes Côtes de Beaune" (red and white wines). Wines with these names are fairly simple versions of Burgundy, but they are affordable.

For a list of the principal villages in the Côte de Beaune, see

Burgundy's famous Hospices de Beaune.

the table on Translating Place Name into Grape Variety, pages 42-57. The *Grand Cru* vineyards of the Côte de Beaune lie in two clusters. One is in the north around the village of Corton and produces red and white wines. The other is in the southern end, in the villages of Chassagne-Montrachet and Puligny-Montrachet. This group of *Grand Cru* vineyards produces white wines only. The famous Montrachet vineyard, which makes what is considered to be the finest version of Chardonnay in the world, is located in the southern cluster.

CÔTE CHALONNAISE

The Côte Chalonnaise is clustered around the town of Chalon, in the center of the Burgundy region. The district appellation here is "Bourgogne Côte Chalonnaise." In addition there are five village names that can be used as the name of a Chalonnaise wine if the grapes were grown within that village. The villages are Bouzeron, Givry, Mercurey, Montagny, and Rully. The general consensus about Côte Chalonnaise wines is that they offer sound Burgundy (Pinot Noir or Chardonnay) characteristics without a high price tag.

The village-level wine of Rully.

CÔTE DE NUITS

The Côte de Nuits is the most northerly of the Burgundy districts, other than the separate district of Chablis. This is primarily Pinot Noir country, though some Chardonnays are also made. Wines made from grapes from around the core of the district are labeled as "Côte de Nuits Villages." The name "Hautes Côtes de Nuits" is given to wines made from grapes grown in the outlying areas. Those wines are not as full-bodied or as ripe in their fruit characteristics.

For a list of the principal villages in the Côte de Nuits, see the table on Translating Place Name into Grape Variety, pages 42-57. All twenty-four of the Grand Cru vineyards in the Côte de Nuits produce red wines. They are produced in very small quantities, making them rare and very expensive. For many, they represent the epitome of Pinot Noir, with floral and truffle aromas, firm but lingering fruit, and a smooth, silky texture.

MACONNAIS

Some of the wines of the Maconnais district are very well known to consumers all around the world. This is the home of Macon-Villages and Pouilly-Fuissé, wines that have been exported to the far corners of the world for decades. The district produces both red and

A typical sight in La Mâconnais.

white lightweight, but enjoyable, wines under the district appellation names of "Macon" or "Macon-Villages." The village of Pouilly-Fuissé produces only white wines—these are usually a bit fuller-bodied and more full-flavored than the district wines. Another reliable but lighter white wine village appellation is Saint-Véran.

Champagne

For most people, Champagne from France represents the height of sparkling wine luxury. The producers here are very adamant that the word Champagne should be used only for the wines from this region. In terms of appellations, Champagne is the only one used, though a village

name may appear on the label if all of the grapes came from vineyards within that village.

If the words *Grand Cru* or *Premier Cru* appear on a label of Champagne, that indicates that the grapes all came from a village that has been rated as *Premier* or *Grand Cru.* All of the vineyards in those villages are presumed to be of the same standard.

In any legal sense, the word Champagne on a French bottle of wine means that the wine is sparkling, that it was made according a particular technique called the *Méthode Champenoise* (Champagne Method), and that the wine maker used one or more of the following grape types: Chardonnay, Pinot Noir, and Pinot Meunier. Note that Pinot Noir and Pinot Meunier are red grapes, and that most Champagne is white. Champagne is one of the best examples in the world that white wine can be made from red grapes.

Most Champagne wines are blends of the three grape types, and blends of several different years, making them non-vintage wines. If the wine is made using only Chardonnay grapes, it is usually identified as *Blanc de Blancs* (white wine from white grapes). The term *Blanc de Noirs* (white from black/red grapes) would indicate a Champagne made from one or both red grapes.

The whole concept of non-vintage Champagne from any producer is to create a high quality sparkling wine that offers the same characteristics to consumers every time they buy the product. That means there should be no variation caused by different weather conditions during the growing season. If a Champagne company feels that one single year provided outstanding growing conditions, they will probably

The notations in the bottom left corner of this Champagne label identify it as a Blanc de Blancs from vineyards in one of the Grand Cru villages of Champagne.

produce a vintage Champagne that year. But it will be noticeably different from the standard non-vintage wines. The whole idea of a vintage Champagne is to showcase that one single year as extraordinary.

The basic steps in the Champagne method are as follows:

1. Several base wines are made from the most recent harvest of grapes. This may mean making several different white Pinot Noir wines from grapes from different locations, several different Chardonnay wines from grapes from different locations, and so on.
2. Those wines are blended together in whatever the wine maker decides are the desired proportions.
3. Small amounts of wines that have been kept on reserve from previous harvest are then added. The judicious addition of these older wines will enable the wine maker to reproduce the standard blend every time the non-vintage wine is made. The French call these two steps the *assemblage.*
4. A quantity of liquid sugar and yeast is added, and then the blended wine is immediately bottled and sealed with a beer cap closure.
5. The presence of the sugar and yeast will cause a second fermentation to occur inside each bottle. One of the by-products of fermentation is carbon dioxide gas. Because the fermentation takes place inside a closed bottle, the carbon dioxide stays in the wine, and is released—causing the wine to "sparkle"—when the consumer opens the bottle.
6. The closed bottles are then stored on their sides. The yeast particles that caused the fermentation collect on the lower side of the bottle as it lies on its side. The laws for Champagne require that the bottles stay in this position for at least fifteen months for non-vintage

   After the second fermentation has been completed in the bottle, the yeast sediment falls to the bottom.

   Champagne and three years for vintage Champagne. During this time period, the decomposing yeast cells impart a yeasty character to the wine that is often identified as a toasty aroma when the wine is opened. This aging stage will also create a rich smoothness in the wine.
7. The next step, called *rémuage* by the French (riddling in

English), is designed to move the yeast sediment from the side of the bottle into the neck. Traditionally, this was done by hand, but today it is usually a mechanized process that involves the shaking and agitation of the inverted bottle to loosen the sediment from the sides and allow it to fall into the bottle neck.

8. The *dégorgement* (disgorging) step requires keeping the bottle inverted, and chilling about one inch of wine in the bottle neck. This traps the yeast sediment in an ice pellet in the bottle. The bottle is then stood upright and the beer cap removed—the pressure inside the bottle expels the ice pellet and the sediment.

9. The wine is then "finished" with a *dosage* of extra wine to replace that lost in the expulsion of the ice pellet. At this stage, most producers also add a small amount of liquid sugar as a final taste adjustment. Depending on how much sugar is added at this stage, the Champagne will be labeled as one of the following: Extra or Ultra Brut (the driest), Brut, Extra Dry, Sec, Demi-Sec, or Doux (the sweetest).

The Champagne method is widely used by sparkling wine producers all around the world, and many sparkling wine producers in other countries also use the dry or sweet designations listed above.

Loire Valley

This region is large and diverse, producing a range of dry white, sweet white, rosé, red, and sparkling wines from many different grape types. However, there is one unifying factor: Since the climate throughout the valley is cool, all of the wines exhibit typical characteristics of high acidity and a crisp texture. The vineyards line the banks of the Loire River as it flows westward to the Atlantic Ocean, and there are several smaller tributaries flowing into the Loire from the north and south, producing protected valleys that seem ideal for grape growing at this northerly latitude.

The western and eastern extremes of the valley are fairly straightforward in terms of the wines produced. Closest to the ocean, in the west, Muscadet is the main wine produced, whereas the inland, easternmost area is famous for Sauvignon Blancs from the villages of Pouilly and Sancerre.

In the central part of the valley, two grapes stand out, though many others are also grown. The principal white grape is Chenin Blanc, used for dry whites, sweet whites, and sparkling wines, and the main red grape is Cabernet Franc, used for rosés and reds.

MUSCADET

This wine is the ideal simple seafood wine—it is a favorite accompaniment to the oysters and mussels of the region. Muscadet is the local growers' nickname for

the grape, and it has become the name of the wine. It offers light, straightforward characteristics, with something of a mineral aroma and flavor, almost recalling the shells of the seafoods that it goes so well with. There are two basic appellations: "Muscadet," which comes from the area directly to the south of the port city of Nantes at the western edge of the Loire Valley, and "Muscadet de Sèvre-et-Maine" from the *département* of Sèvre et Maine to the west of Nantes. The latter should be a little more full-bodied and full-flavored.

The word Muscadet has no relationship to Muscat—the wines are made from different grapes and Muscat is almost always sweet and heavy, while Muscadet is always dry and light.

POUILLY AND SANCERRE

These two villages specialize in dry white wines made from Sauvignon Blanc. They are usually medium-bodied wines with green fruit characteristics, a slight mineral, wet rock aroma, and high, tart acidity. The wines from Sancerre are named after the village and will be identified as "Appellation Sancerre Contrôlée," whereas the wines from the village of Pouilly are labeled as

"Pouilly-Fumé," because the local growers refer to the Sauvignon Blanc grape as the Blanc Fumé. This is the origin of the term Fumé Blanc, used by some United States producers as a synonym for Sauvignon Blanc.

There is also a red wine called Sancerre made from Pinot Noir grapes. It is generally lighter in body and higher in acidity than the Pinot Noir wines of Burgundy.

The appellation contrôlée laws for white wine from the village of Sancerre require that the wine be made from Sauvignon Blanc grapes.

CENTRAL LOIRE VALLEY

Chenin Blanc wines: Not many places in the world specialize in the Chenin Blanc grape variety, but the Central Loire Valley has been home to this grape for hundreds of years, and some fascinating wines can be found here. It is the basis for many dry, sweet, and sparkling white wines. The usual varietal characteristics of melon and a slight nuttiness can be found in any of the examples of Chenin from here, though the flavors and aromas are most delicate in the sparkling versions, and strongest in the sweet wines.

The most frequently seen dry versions of Loire Valley Chenin Blanc wines come from the village appellations of Anjou Blanc, Saumur Blanc, Savennières, and Vouvray. Of those, Savennières is the finest example, with far more complexity and ripe fruit character than the other examples. Within the village of Savennières there are two *Grand Cru* vineyards: Château de la Roche aux Moines, and Coulée de Serrant. Wines from either one of those vineyards will have the

name of the vineyard on the label. They are expensive wines, but exceptional examples of Chenin Blanc at its best.

Sweet Chenin Blanc wines from this area achieve their sweetness either because they are late harvest wines, or because the grapes have been dehydrated by the onset of the Botrytis mold. Because the Loire Valley is a cool climate, the sweet wines from here retain very high levels of acidity, which means that these wines display a very attractive liveliness and crispness, with none of the cloying character that can be found in some sweet wines.

Depending on where the grapes were grown, a sweet Chenin Blanc will be named as any of the following: Bonnezeaux, Coteaux du Layon, Montlouis, Quarts de Chaume, or Vouvray. Of those, Montlouis and Vouvray produce the lightest, simplest versions, whereas Bonnezeaux and Quarts de Chaume are both *Grand Cru* vineyards that make much more complex, flavorful wines. While this is not always the case, many sweet Loire Valley wines can be identified as sweet by the word *moëlleux* on the label.

Sparkling wines from this area are made by the Champagne method, and offer a light, crisp style, with citrus fruit character. They are a less expensive alternative to some of the pricier sparkling wines from around the world, and they are good quality. The most frequently seen appellations are Cremant de la Loire, and Saumur Mousseux. As a general note, "Cremant" is a term used to denote French sparkling wine made outside the region of Champagne.

CENTRAL LOIRE VALLEY

Cabernet Franc Wines: Although several other red grapes are grown in the Central Loire Valley, most notably Cabernet Sauvignon and Gamay, it is the Cabernet Franc that gives a distinctive character to the red wines of this region. Produced from grapes grown in this cool climate, the wines display the hallmark high acidity of the region along with a fresh, red berry character. Their medium body and appealing fruitiness make them prime candidates for summertime drinking with lighter foods and casual backyard cooking.

The appellations used for red wines from here are Anjou Rouge, Bourgueil, Chinon, and Saumur-Champigny. The first is a regional appellation, whereas the last three names denote that the wine came from a village appellation. Those village wines usually display riper fruit elements and a little more complexity.

The appellation name used for Central Loire semi-sweet rosé is Cabernet d'Anjou, whereas the dry version is called Rosé de la Loire. Both are light and simple, but charming wines.

Rhône Valley

The Rhône region is one of France's hotter regions, famous more for red wines than white, as is often the case in warm grape growing areas. For those red wines, the most commonly used grape varieties are Syrah, Grenache, and Mourvèdre. However, there is a distinction between wines from the northern part of the Rhône Valley, where Syrah is the dominant grape, and those from the southern Rhône Valley, where Grenache is more widely planted.

For white wines from the northern Rhône, the Viognier grape type is used for two distinct appellations, whereas other areas tend to produce a blend from the Marsanne and Roussanne grape types. In the southern Rhône, Marsanne and Roussanne are used in small quantities along with the more common Clairette and Grenache Blanc.

As in other regions of France, the Rhône Valley has regional appellations and village appellations. The two regional appellations are Côtes-du-Rhône, and Côtes-du-Rhône-Villages. The red wines from these regional appellations are usually blends of the three main red grapes, and are made as light- to medium-bodied wines with attractive red fruit characteristics. The village appellations are highlighted in the Northern Rhône Valley and Southern Rhône Valley sections that follow.

NORTHERN RHÔNE VALLEY

The red wines from this part of the valley are usually 100 percent Syrah, making them full-flavored, robust wines with lots of complexity and intense, dark fruit characteristics. Some of them are capable of aging for several years. The village appellations that are most well known for these fine Syrah wines are Cornas, Côte-Rôtie, Crozes-Hermitage, Hermitage, and St-Joseph. Of those, the finest examples, in order of reputation, come from Hermitage, Côte-Rôtie, and Cornas.

The red wine from Crozes-Hermitage is made from the Syrah grape.

The white wines of the Château Grillet and Condrieu appellations are made from Viognier grapes, while small quantities of white wine are made as Marsanne-Roussanne blends in the appellations of Crozes-Hermitage, Hermitage, and St-Joseph.

SOUTHERN RHÔNE VALLEY

Several different grape varieties are permitted in the appellations of the southern Rhône, but most of the reds are blends of Grenache, Syrah, and Mourvèdre. The most widely used white varieties are Clairette, Grenache Blanc, Marsanne, and Roussanne.

The most famous village appellation here is Châteauneuf-du-Pape, making both red and white wines that offer ripe, abundant fruit flavors and medium levels of acidity. Two other village appellations with a good reputation are Gigondas and Vacqueyras, both of which concentrate on red wine production.

There are two other famous wines from the southern Rhône Valley. One is the rosé wine from the village appellation Tavel. It is unfortunate that a lot of people do not regard rosé wine as "serious" because a well-made Tavel is a treat of ripe, red plum fruit and crisp acidity. The other "different" wine is the Muscat de Beaumes-de-Venise. This is a sweet wine made from Muscat grapes. The juice is allowed to begin

This label is for the sweet white wine made from Muscat grapes grown in the village of Beaumes de Venise.

to ferment, but then brandy is added to stop the fermentation, leaving lots of natural, fresh grape sugars in the wine. The use of brandy to stop the fermentation brings the alcohol level up to around 15 percent. The village name of Beaumes-de-Venise can also be used as an appellation for red wine.

THE SOUTH COAST

The broad sweep of land that curves from the Pyrénées mountains in the west, all the way around to the border with Italy combines sun, rugged mountains, green valleys, and clear blue skies. This expansive area produces enormous quantities of wine, though only a small amount of it qualifies for Appellation Contrôlée status because the grapes are not part of the authorized list, or they are being grown in unauthorized areas. The majority of the wines fall into the Vin de Pays category, which in some ways is an advantage because it means that there are not regulations about how the wine should be named. As a result, many of these wines reach the market with a simple varietal name on the label. This means that they compete directly with the varietal label wines from Australia, the United States, and elsewhere.

The two biggest Vin de Pays areas that export all around the world are the Vin de Pays d'Oc, and the Vin de Pays de l'Hérault. Both these areas make sound, inexpensive single varietal wines such as Chardonnay, Syrah, Merlot, and Cabernet Sauvignon.

For Appellation Contrôlée level wines, there are two large regional appellations, the Coteaux du Languedoc and the Côtes du Rousillon. Both these appellations produce mostly red wines from the basic combination of Grenache, Syrah, and Mourvèdre—also known as the GSM blend—though both areas are required to include a large proportion of a grape called Cinsaut as well.

The smaller appellations of Minervois and St-Chinian produce red wines from the same GSM blend, again with Carignan added. Minervois wines are the leaner of the two, reflective perhaps of the dry terrain and sparse vegetation, whereas St-Chinian wines are flashier, and more generous with their flavors.

Italy

Learning about Italian wines presents a special challenge, simply because a huge diversity of wine types is produced from innumerable (often unfamiliar) grape types in every corner of the nation. The best approach to Italian wines is to pare them down to the bare minimum, and to familiarize yourself with three major regions (out of  a total of twenty) that all produce world-class wines and are frequently found on the export market. The basics of Italian wine demand some insight into the country's appellation system, and a knowledge of how the wines are named. The three regions to look at are Piedmont, Tuscany, and Veneto.

Appellation System

Where the French talk of Appellation d'Origine Contrôlée, the Italians refer to their system of *Denominazione di Origine Controllata* (DOC). Both phrases mean the same thing—controlled naming of origin—and both systems stipulate specific grape types to be used in a defined region. The Italians talk of DOC zones rather than appellations. In all of Italy's regions, there are close to 250 DOC zones, producing almost 900 different wines.

There are two other important categories in the Italian wine system. The first is *DOCG (Denominazione di Origine Controllata e Garantita)* where the implication is that wines awarded this status are somehow very special. They may be special from the perspective of perceived quality, they may be important, or they may simply be very famous. There are currently twenty-four DOCG wines in Italy. Most of them come from, again, the three regions of Piedmont, Tuscany, and Veneto.

If a wine has been produced according to all the regulations of a DOC or DOCG zone, the full phrase—not the acronym—will be printed on the label.

The second additional category is called *IGT (Indicazione Geografica Tipica)*, suggesting a wine that is somehow typical of its geographic origin. This category was introduced to cover a large number of high quality wines that were being produced from unauthorized grape types and therefore didn't qualify for DOC or DOCG status. Many of these wines have been referred to as "Super Tuscans" because they are produced from grapes grown in Tuscany, but those grapes do not fit the DOC model of which grapes may be used.

If we add the growing number of IGT wines to the list, there are easily more than a thousand wines from Italy that deserve attention!

Italian Wine Names

Most Italian wines are named according to one of four formats: place name, grape variety name, grape and place name, or proprietary name.

PLACE NAME

A place name on an Italian wine label indicates that the wine is from an approved DOC or DOCG zone, and that approved grape types have been used to make the wine. Just about everybody knows one or two Italian place name wines,

This Italian DOC label identifies the wine as made from Pinot Grigio grapes, grown in the Valdadige region near Venice.

although the fact that they are place names may not be obvious.

Some of the more famous place names used for Italian wines are Chianti, Barolo, Soave, and Asti.

GRAPE VARIETY NAME

The most obvious candidate here is Pinot Grigio, now a very familiar item in wine stores all around the world. Other examples include Teroldego, Tocai Friulano, and Nero d'Avola.

GRAPE AND PLACE NAME

This is perhaps the most useful format since it provides information on the grape type and the region of origin. The name is usually three words long, with the first word being the grape type, and

This label indicates the wine is made from Barbera grapes grown in Monferrato.

the third word being the place. The middle word is *di* or *d'*, meaning "from." Well-known examples are Moscato d'Asti, Dolcetto d'Alba, and Barbera d'Asti.

PROPRIETARY NAME

The number of wines using this naming format has increased dramatically with the growing number of IGT wines that do not conform to DOC regulations. Some famous examples include Tignanello, Sassoaloro, and Luce. As with any proprietary name anywhere in the world, the problem with such names is that they do not convey any information about the grape type or types used to make the wine.

Other Useful Terms

Three useful terms in understanding Italian wine labels are *Classico, Riserva,* and *Superiore.* The inclusion of the word *Classico* in a wine name indicates that the grapes were grown in a smaller section of the DOC zone. The *Classico* area is usually the original grape growing area within a zone. Examples with DOC or

DOCG zones that have a *Classico* section are Chianti and Soave.

The word *Riserva* on an Italian label indicates that the wine was aged for a specific period of time in oak barrels. The exact length of time in the barrel is stipulated in the DOC or DOCG regulations, and it varies from zone to zone.

There is a presumed implication that that wines labeled as *Classico* or *Riserva* are somehow "better" than wines without those terms on the label. Whereas this is most often the case, demonstrated by fuller, riper flavors and more complexity, it should be remembered that in the purest sense, the term *Classico* is merely a geographic notation, and the term *Riserva* simply indicates more aging.

The *Superiore* notation indicates that the wine must have a minimum alcohol level that is at least 1 percent higher than that of the regular (non-*Superiore*) version of the same wine. (The same is true for the term *Supérieur* in France.)

The Wines of Piedmont

In northwestern Italy, where the Alpine foothills ease southward to the Ligurian coast and the Italian mainland peninsula, the region of Piedmont enjoys the sunny summer days and cool breezes of the Po river valley system. Despite the industrialization of cities like Turin, the landscape is dotted with innumerable signs that the people of Piedmont love their food and wine, from Arborio rice, to peppers, salami, and the highly prized white truffle. The many hilltop villages, with their inevitable church tower, could easily be mistaken for the guardians of the slopes that are home to some of Italy's finest vineyards.

As a relatively cool region, Piedmont has always been revered for producing wines with clean flavors and sharp acidity. Most of the wines are red, but there are a few notable whites. Among the whites, the two most important grape varieties are Cortese and Moscato.

The Cortese grape produces a crisp, light- to medium-bodied wine with citrus and green apple

Vineyards cover the slopes below the hilltop towns in the region of Piedmont.

notes. It can be labeled as Cortese di Gavi, or just Gavi (after the village of Gavi). If all of the grapes came from the small area immediately surrounding the village, the wine will be called Gavi di Gavi. All three versions qualify for DOCG status.

The most famous product of the Moscato grape variety is the wine that's now officially called simply Asti, though millions of consumers still refer to it as Asti Spumante. This sparkling, sweet wine is well liked for its low alcohol level, peach aroma, and ripe fruit flavor.

A very similar wine is called Moscato d'Asti, though it is only just fizzy, as opposed to sparkling, and is often sweeter than straight Asti. Both versions of the wine have DOCG status.

Piedmont boasts a number of red DOCG wines, including Barbaresco, Barolo, Gattinara, and Ghemme, all made from the Nebbiolo grape. The Nebbiolo is a highly revered variety that's considered capable of producing some very fine wines, especially when it's grown in the villages of Barolo and Barbaresco. At their best, these wines display a very complex profile of ripe red fruit with a slightly perfumed tea aroma and hints of earth or leather. The wines are also marked by high acidity and substantial tannins that take a few years to soften out.

All Barolo and Barbaresco wines are aged in wood, but the precise method of aging has become the subject of much debate. The traditional method would be to use large casks with many years

DOES IT SPARKLE OR FIZZ?

Any wine with a noticeable stream of effervescence in the glass contains varying levels of carbon dioxide gas that have been trapped in the wine during the fermentation process. A wine is said to be fully sparkling when it has around seven atmospheres of pressure inside the bottle (one atmosphere is equivalent to fourteen pounds per square inch). Sparkling wines generally show a generous stream of bubbles in the glass, and they create a noticeable tingling sensation on the tongue.

A wine would be referred to as fizzy if it has only three to four atmospheres of pressure. The bubbles in the glass are more dispersed, and the effect in the mouth is more frothy than prickly.

The amount of effervescence in the wine can be controlled by the wine maker by shortening or prolonging the fermentation process. The longer the fermentation, the more carbon dioxide is produced.

of aging, but modernists argue that this produces a wine that is far too hard and tannic, even after many subsequent years of bottle aging have precipitated those harsh tannins in the form of sediment in the bottle. The new method is to use small, new barrels for the wood-aging process, generally resulting in a wine with fewer hard tannins and more generous fruit up front on the palate. Is one way "better" than the other? It's all a matter of taste and fashion.

One other DOCG wine from Piedmont is the fun and frothy Brachetto d'Acqui, a sweet, sparkling red wine that exudes ripe strawberry aromas and flavors.

In addition to those DOCG red wines, there are two other important Piedmontese red grapes that produce red wines of DOC status—Barbera and Dolcetto. Most of the wines made from these grapes lean toward medium-bodied versions with fresh, lively fruit up front, though some producers make fuller-bodied versions with noticeable wood character that is derived from aging in barrels. There are various DOC zones for these wines, but the best ones are Dolcetto d'Alba and Barbera d'Alba.

The Wines of Tuscany

The region of Tuscany has been romanticized and idealized for centuries, probably with good reason. Lying to the west of the Appennine spine of Italy, the land undulates gently down to the west until it reaches the Mediterranean Sea. Culturally, the area is dominated by the walled city of Florence, heart of the Italian Renaissance. In the center of Tuscany's wine lands is the equally inspiring and historic city of Siena, approximately 100 miles north of Rome. For decades, the Tuscan wine scene was equated with Chianti, but the modern picture is much more complex. Chianti is still a major player, but its fine wines are now complemented by an array of worthy newcomers.

In Tuscany, the Sangiovese grape reigns supreme. Depending on exactly where it is grown, this variety can produce very attractive but simple wines, as well as very fine, complex, structured wines that demand serious attention. There are five DOCG wines based on Sangiovese in Tuscany: They are Brunello di Montalcino, Carmignano, Chianti, Chianti Classico, and Vino Nobile di Montepulciano.

Of those, Chianti is the simplest, with bright, clean fruit flavors of sour cherry, and a light aroma of woodland flowers, like violets. At the other end of the scale is the Brunello di Montalcino, where the cherry character is still evident, but as dried cherries or dark bing cherries—it is much more emphatic and extensive, with definite woodsy notes and hints of tea and licorice. The difference is like hearing a Mozart melody played on the flute, and then hearing the fully orchestrated version: There is a family resemblance between the two, but in the latter everything is amplified and enhanced.

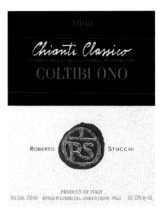

There are also many DOC and IGT wines from Tuscany that are based solely or partly on the Sangiovese grape type. The IGT wines include any number of "Super Tuscans" with proprietary names like Le Pergole Torte or Sassoalloro. Simple DOC Sangiovese wines include Rosso di Montalcino and Rosso di Montepulciano.

Tuscany is also proud to be home to a white DOCG wine that has been produced here for centuries. That wine is the refreshing Vernaccia di San Gimignano (Vernaccia grapes from the vineyards around the medieval hill town of San Gimignano, about an hour outside of Florence).

The Wines of Veneto

The Veneto region in northwestern Italy, near Venice, has long been known on the export markets for three famous wines—the white Soave and the reds Valpolicella and Bardolino. Unfortunately, much of what was exported in previous decades was not of the highest quality, but nowadays these wines deserve closer attention. Modern Soave is an attractive medium-bodied white wine with ripe apple notes and a sort of almond background. It certainly deserves a better reputation than a good wine to cook with, a fact that is reflected in the recent promotion of the Soave Superiore and Soave Classico wines to DOCG level. The main grape type is Garganega.

Similarly, Valpolicella has been transformed from a simple, light wine to one of more substance, still with vibrant ripe fruit, but with a richer quality to it. The main grape types are Corvina, Molinara, and Rondinella.

Some Soave and Valpolicella producers also market limited quantities of a regional specialty called Recioto. It is produced by harvesting the grapes and allowing them to dry on racks before the wine making process starts. The result is a rich, sweet wine in both cases, referred to, respectively, as Recioto di Soave and Recioto di Valpolicella. The Recioto di Soave version has been awarded DOCG status.

Using the same process, it is also possible to end up with a drier version of Valpolicella, called simply Amarone, or Amarone di Valpolicella. This rich, full-bodied wine has distinct dried fruit aromas, concentrated flavors, with high alcohol and substantial tannins.

The light red Bardolino wines have a similar grape type composition to Valpolicella, i.e. mostly Corvina and Molinara, but no Rondinella. These wines are particularly refreshing with their bright color, lightly perfumed aroma, and fresh cherry flavors. The *Superiore* and *Classico* versions of Bardolino have been awarded DOCG status.

Other DOCG Wines of Italy

The Piedmont, Tuscan, and Veneto regions are home to sixteen of the twenty-four DOCG wines of Italy. The remaining DOCG wines—from other areas—are listed below.

From the region of Lombardy come some impressive red

Nebbiolo-based wines, collectively referred to as Valtellina Superiore. An additional notation on the label will identify the wine as coming from one of the four zones within Lombardy: Grumello, Inferno, Sassella, or Valgella. The region is also home to sparkling white and rosé DOCG wines called Franciacorta.

Located to the southeast of Tuscany, the region of Umbria has two red DOCG wines: Torgiano Rosso Riserva, based mostly on Sangiovese grapes; and the Sagrantino di Montefalco, made from Sagrantino grapes.

A recently announced DOCG wine, Ramandolo, is a dessert wine made from the Verduzzo grape type from the region of Friuli-Venezia-Giulia. The famous food region of Emilia-Romagna—which is known for its sweet balsamic vinegar and nutty Parmigiano-Reggiano, among other treats—is home to Italy's first DOCG wine, called Albana di Romagna.

In the southern region of Campania, a red wine called Taurasi (made from Aglianico grapes) has DOCG status, and from the island of Sardinia comes a fresh, delightful white wine called Vermentino di Gallura.

Spain

Through the 1980s and '90s, the Spanish wine industry seemed to be making up for lost time following the nation's effective political and economic isolation caused by General Franco's fascist dictatorship. At that time, Spain's wine makers were far behind the rest of the world in terms of technological advances, like the universal use of stainless-steel fermentation vats. Spain was also woefully lacking in the area of wine legislation for the use of place names, permitted grape types, and so on. However, in the last quarter century, it has become a modern European nation, leaving behind its tired, oxidized wine styles of a bygone age, and emerging as the proud producer of stylish, even progressive, wines that have consumers all around the world taking a second look.

To coincide with the modernization of the industry and laws, Spain has been actively promoting wines from its many different appellations. At one time, Spain's most famous wine might have

been Sherry (from the Jerez region), or Rioja (from the region of the same name), but today there is much competition for recognition from other regions.

The wine regions that are currently receiving critical acclaim all fall under the appellation system known as *Denominacion de Origen*, and that phrase or the initials DO will appear on the label if a wine was produced from the permitted grapes grown within the stated region. So far, one region, Rioja, has been awarded the higher status of *Denominacion de Origen Calificada*, or DOC. The most important DOs are Jerez, Penedès, Priorat, Rias Baixas, Ribera del Duero, Rioja, and Rueda.

Jerez

The DO of Jerez is situated in the historic province of Andalucia, a dry, sunny area that is the flamboyant home of bullfights, flamenco, and Moorish history. The standard wine from such a hot location would generally be dull and uninteresting, but the Jerezanos, with a good deal of foreign input, have created one of the world's most enduring and endearing drinks: It is known as Sherry, the Anglicized form of the regional name Jerez.

The Palomino grape.

Sherry is basically a dry white wine, made from the Palomino grape variety, that is fortified and then aged in wooden barrels with a small air space in the barrel to encourage oxidation. From there, different styles of Sherry naturally emerge depending on whether or not a layer of natural local yeast grows on the surface of the wine, thereby decelerating the oxidation process. This yeast is known as *flor*, and it settles on the surface of the wine in some barrels but not in others. There are three main styles of Sherry that come from this process: *Fino* (with the subcategory *Manzanilla*), *Amontillado*, and *Oloroso*.

Where *flor* occurs in great quantity, completely covering the surface of the wine, the oxidation rate slows down dramatically. As a result, the wine will stay relatively pale in color, with a delicate, Brazil nut aroma and flavor characteristic. This style of Sherry is known as *Fino*, or, if the style is particularly delicate, it will be called *Manzanilla*. If a small amount of *flor* grows in patches on the wine, oxidation will continue slowly, creating a light tawny color and a richer, almond aroma and flavor in a wine known as *Amontillado*. Where there is no growth or very little growth of *flor*, oxidation continues at full pace, turning the wine dark brown with walnut characteristics. This wine is known as *Oloroso*.

When each barrel has been categorized as one of the above styles, the wine will be added to a *solera*, which serves as an automatic blending and aging system. In simple terms, a *solera* is a stack of barrels, made up of several rows, in which each barrel contains the same style of Sherry. On average, there are ten rows in a *solera*. When it is time to bottle a particular style of Sherry, a small portion of that style is drawn from every barrel in the bottom row. The space

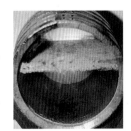

Flor growing in a cask of fino Sherry.

created in those barrels is then filled with wine drawn from every barrel in the second row. When wine is taken from every barrel in the top row to fill the space in the row beneath it, new categorized wine is added to each barrel in the top row. This system results in a consistent product for each style of Sherry that any producer markets, although small adjustments for color can be made as a final step.

Fino and *Manzanilla* sherries are left bone dry, and they are most often used as aperitif drinks. *Amontillado* can be dry, or very lightly sweetened. The full, rich *Oloroso* sherries are sometimes left dry, but can also be sweetened: A sweet *Oloroso* is sometimes

VINTAGE AND AGING TERMINOLOGY

Any one of the DOs in Spain may incorporate certain approved and defined words on the label to provide the consumer with an indication of how long the wine has been aged before being released onto the market. Useful terms include the following:

- *Cosecha* – The Spanish word for vintage.
- *Crianza* – A minimum of six months' aging in small oak barrels plus two years bottle aging. In the regions of Rioja and Ribera del Duero, the requirement is a minimum of one-year barrel aging plus one year in bottle.
- *Reserva* – At least two years aging for white wines, including six months in barrels, and at least three years aging for reds, including one year in barrel.
- *Gran Reserva* – At least four years aging for whites, including six months in barrels, and at least five years for reds, three in the barrel and two in the bottle.

As in Italy, the inclusion of aging terms on the label is not a guarantee of better quality, but there is usually a positive correlation.

labeled as a Cream Sherry. The sweetening is often done by adding small portions of sweet wine made from the extra sweet Pedro Ximenez or Moscatel grape varieties. As a rare treat, a few producers make an exceptionally sweet Sherry labeled as Pedro Ximenez since it is made exclusively from that grape variety.

Penedès

The region of Penedès lies southwest of the vibrant Catalonian capital, Barcelona. It is the birthplace of Cava, the sparkling wine that's made according to the French *méthode Champenoise*.

Penedès is large enough to encompass three distinct subregions, the coolest of which is at fairly high elevations in the interior Catalan mountain range, where many of the grapes for the sparkling Cava are grown. Coming down from the mountains to the coastal plains, the temperatures rise, allowing for warmer climate grape varieties such as Tempranillo and Garnacha.

On the export market, Penedès has something of a one-sided reputation. It is often seen as the center of a revolution in growing non-traditional grapes, especially French varieties such as Cabernet Sauvignon, Merlot, Pinot Noir, Sauvignon Blanc, and Chardonnay, which are bottled as single varietal wines or blends. While this may be true of the progressive producers like the Torres family and Jean Léon, there are plenty of traditionalists who continue to work on the customary red and white blended wines from Tempranillo and Garnacha (for reds) and Parellada, Macabeo, and Xarello (for whites).

The use of the term Cava indicates a Champagne-method sparkling wine made from specific grape types. The traditional grape types are Macabeo, Parellada, and Xarello, but many Cava producers are now including varying amounts of Chardonnay in the blend. Without the Chardonnay, most Cava wines were easily distinguishable from other sparkling wines because of their noticeably lower acidity and slight earthy quality. The inclusion of Chardonnay in the blend, as well as advances in stainless-steel wine making technology, have resulted in increasingly fresh and lively wines that can be very attractive, especially given their price, which falls somewhere in the $8.00 to $25.00 range. Some of the most well-known Cava brands are Freixenet, Codorniu, and Segura Viudas.

Priorat

To the east of Penedès, within the larger DO of Tarragona lies the small mountainous DO called Priorat, previously known as Priorato. Here the southeast- and south-facing slopes are ideal for catching and trapping the full impact of the sun's warmth, which is stored in the rocky soil of the vineyards and provides radiant heat later in the day, thereby intensifying the ripening process. The results are Garnacha (Grenache) and Carignan grapes with intense flavors and substantial tannins making full-bodied, robust red wines that can take several years to soften up.

Rias Baixas

In the northwestern corner of Spain lies the province of Galicia, an area famous for its holy site of Santiago de Compostella, its rugged coastline with several deep fjords (*rias* in Spanish), and its cool, even cold, blustery weather. It is far from the warm, sunny images that the mention of Spain usually evokes. One of the

A vineyard in Rias Baixas.

bright new stars in the Spanish wine heavens is the DO of Rias Baixas, a cool growing region that has bounced onto the international market with its fresh, lively, and very appealing white wines based completely or mostly on the Albarino grape type. Like many cool growing areas, the Rias Baixas DO is capable of extracting clean, fresh, apricot and peach flavors in the wine, balanced by sharp but attractive acidity. Labeled as Albarino, the wine is required to be 100 percent of that grape type. If the wine is labeled as Rias Baixas, the Albarino content must be a minimum of 70 percent.

Ribera del Duero

Much of central Spain is an upland plateau, dominated by the capital city Madrid. About 100 miles north of Madrid lies the Ribera del Duero DO, with its vineyards dotted on the valley slopes of the Duero river. This is the home of two Spanish heroes; El Cid, who liberated Spain from Moorish occupation; and Vega Sicilia, a pioneering red wine blended from Tempranillo and the red Bordeaux varieties that put this region on the map in the late 1800s. Today this DO enjoys an international reputation for its red Tempranillo wines, which are sometimes blended with small quantities of Garnacha. The best Ribera del Duero reds show intense, dark, plummy fruit with firm but not overly astringent tannins when young. Left to age, the tannins soften to provide a profile of generous ripe, dark fruit and velvety smoothness.

Rioja

About 100 miles southwest of the Pyrénées mountains that form the border with France lies the Rioja region. Indeed, the Pyrénées can arguably be said to have an influence on the area since the western end of Rioja is composed largely of steep-sided fertile river valleys fed by the snow melting from the mountains. As the Rioja region continues southeastward along the Ebro river valley, the land becomes flatter with sparser, scrubby vegetation. It is the more mountainous northwestern section of Rioja, known as Rioja Alta, that is the more highly regarded for growing Tempranillo and Granacha, which are usually blended together to make Rioja's great red wines.

Producers who use a higher percentage of Tempranillo usually make their wine in what is called a *Clarete* style, which tends to be a bit harder in tannins, with more focused, concentrated dark fruit character. Clarete Rioja wines are traditionally bottled in the cylindrical Bordeaux-shaped bottle, which has a pronounced shoulder at the base of the neck. Red Rioja wines that use a higher percentage of Garnacha are referred to as Tinto, indicating a

A Riserva label for Rioja wine.

softer texture, and more of the typical red plum preserve flavors of Garnacha. They are usually bottled in a Rhône- or Burgundy-shaped bottle, with sloping shoulders.

Oak aging has always played an important role in the formation of Rioja wines, since the Rioja producers have long felt that their wines should be enjoyable when released onto the market, without the need for further aging. Traditionally, producers used large, old casks for fermentation and aging, but the current practice calls for stainless-steel vats for fermentation and new or one-year-old small barrels for aging. Like many Spanish wine producers, the Rioja wine makers prefer American oak barrels because they seem to impart a softer character to the wine.

Historically, Rioja produced white wines. The few producers who continue this practice today have maintained a more or less historic style with an obvious oxidized, nutty note in the aroma and flavor of the wine. This makes the wine seem listless and dull compared to the modern, vibrant versions from places like Rias Baixas. A number of producers who used to make white wine in Rioja have shifted their white wine focus to the Rueda DO.

Rueda

To the west of Ribera del Duero, still on the northern edge of Spain's upland plateau, the Rueda region experiences a similar climate of warm summers and cold winters. And, like Ribera del Duero, Rueda is steeped in history—it is the home of Don Quixote's creator, Cervantes, and the burial site of Columbus. Despite massive investments in the early 1970s and the granting of DO status in 1980, recognition was slow to come. But this DO is now enjoying the attention paid to its white wines, especially the fresh and lively stainless steel fermented versions made from the Verdejo grape type that display clean, ripe yellow plum aromas and a hint of perfume.

Portugal

The nation of Portugal has long been famous for the production of the fortified wine known as Port (or Porto). The positive aspect of this is that port wines are now enjoyed in most countries around the world. The downside is that other Portuguese wines have languished in the shadows. Recent years have seen a concerted effort by the Portuguese government to promote all of the nation's wines, not just the highly regarded port.

The Portuguese appellation system is known as *Denominacao de Origem Controlada* (denominations of controlled origin), and like other European appellation systems, the key elements of the system are to regulate geographic growing areas and grape varieties used. According to European law, when a grape name is used on a label, it means that at least 80 percent of that grape must be used to make the wine, though any wine maker is free to use more than the minimum. The primary appellations to consider are Dao, Douro, and Vinho Verde. Also, the use of the word Reserva on a Portuguese label indicates that specific aging requirements have been met for that wine.

Dao

A terraced vineyard in Dao.

The terraced vineyards that dot the landscape in this region look very orderly, even romantic, but they are the product of many years of arduous manual labor. They are necessary on the steeper, high elevation vineyards in the interior mountainous section of the region because they prevent erosion and make it possible to tend to the vines. In the flatter, more westerly areas, there is less need for the terraces. As an inland area, this appellation enjoys warm growing conditions that allow for easy ripening of the grapes. The red version of Dao wine relies on the Touriga Nacional grape for a full, ripe style, with hints of a floral, perfumed aroma, though five other red grapes are permitted in the blend. The best versions of white Dao show a distinctly nutty aroma that is the hallmark of the Encruzado grape variety (one of the four authorized grape types). One of the distinctive features of all Dao wines is their remarkable softness.

Douro

Terraced vineyards are even more commonplace in the Douro region that stretches from the west coast port town of Oporto eastwards to the rugged mountains that mark the boundary with Spain. The lower coastal region enjoys moderately warm

temperatures, average rainfall, and fertile soils that provide for lush, green vegetation and vines that thrive fairly easily. Further inland, the climate becomes more arid, and the terrain more rugged, even requiring that, historically, vineyard plots had to be dynamited to make the land workable. The intense summertime heat in the interior produces grapes of extreme ripeness.

Overall, Douro is known for producing mostly red wines with ripe fruit flavors and smooth texture, primarily from the Touriga Nacional and Tinta Roriz grape varieties. Sometimes those grape variety names will show up on the label. Many of the wines have a rich softness that is very appealing. The most famous of the Douro red wines is Barca Velha.

However, Douro is most well known for its Port wines (also called *Porto*), which are sweet and fortified with brandy (it is added as part of the wine making process). A number of different types of Port exist, but there are some common features regardless of style. First, the vast majority of all Port is red. Second, it is always sweet. And third, it is always higher in alcohol than standard wine, often around 20 percent alcohol. Different nations in varying regions of the world enjoy the many permutations of Port for different reasons. For example, the French like to serve Port as an aperitif before dinner, whereas most English-speaking

A typical Douro vineyard.

WHY PORT?

In the late 1700s and early 1800s, a number of British traders settled in various parts of Europe with an eye to developing trade opportunities for the exportation of goods back to England, Scotland, and Ireland. Several wine trade routes emerged from this period. Bordeaux still has a substantial British contingent, as do the Sherry region of Spain and the Port area of Portugal.

The word "Port" is simply derived from the city of Oporto on the west coast of Portugal that served as the shipping point for large quantities of the heavy, rich, sweet wine to be sent back to "the old country."

nations keep Port as a dessert item or an after-dinner drink.

To begin to understand Port, we can start by categorizing it as non-vintage or vintage. The same considerations apply here as to French Champagne, which is also produced as non-vintage or vintage. The majority of all Port is a non-vintage product, achieved by adding small amounts of Port wine from previous years to the current year's production. The aim here is to produce a Port wine that always offers the same experience to the consumer.

If the growing conditions during one single year are extraordinary, then the producers will put out a vintage dated Port from that year. But the whole notion of a vintage dated Port is that it is the exception—it stands alone as a reflection of what was special about that year.

NON-VINTAGE PORT

This category is also referred to as wood-aged Port because all the aging of the wine is done in wooden barrels. When the Port is bottled, it is ready for drinking. Two styles of non-vintage Port exist—ruby and tawny. Non-vintage ruby is a blend of younger wines, usually between four and eight years of age. The youth of the parent wines makes the resulting port a rich ruby

color and lends it fresh, vibrant dark fruit characteristics.

In contrast, non-vintage tawny is a blend of wines that are usually at least seven years old, resulting in a wine with a rich mahogany color and the aromas and flavors of dried fruit. In fact, tawny Ports are an excellent accompaniment to dried fruits and nuts at the end of a meal, whereas the ruby versions pair better with strong cheeses.

Within the tawny category, there are some specialty wines referred to as Indicated Age tawnies. These wines are blended from old wines of different ages, but are designed to reflect the typical characteristics of the Indicated Age on the label. The permitted Indicated Ages are Ten-Year-Old Tawny, Twenty-Year-Old Tawny, Thirty-Year-Old Tawny, and Over-Forty-Year-Old Tawny.

VINTAGE PORT

Produced in very small quantities, this is a highly prized item. As the wine of one single year, there are special regulations that require that the wine be bottled between the second and third year from the date of harvest. In essence, this means that the wine is aged in wood for up to three years and is then bottled while it is still comparatively young, with very high levels of tannin, and an inky black hue. The whole point about vintage dated Port is that it is supposed to be matured in bottle over a very long period of time. The generally recommended time period for aging is fifteen years, but not many people find that they can wait that long.

During the aging period, the wine will throw a heavy sediment, made up of particles of tannin and pigmentation, meaning that vintage Port that has been aged demands decanting, which separates the matured wine from the sediment. (For more on decanting, see the box on pages 136-137.) Even after extensive aging, vintage Port is still a robust wine, with deep color and vibrant fruit, but modified by a refined softness.

LATE BOTTLED VINTAGE PORT

To provide consumers and restaurants with a Port wine that offers some of the characteristics of vintage Port without the hassle of extensive aging and decanting, the Port producers offer Late Bottled Vintage wines. To qualify for Late Bottled status, the wine must be from one single year and bottled between four and six years from the date of harvest. Though they will never be as great or prestigious as vintage Ports, Late Bottled versions offer a viable, less expensive alternative. Most producers bottle them in a ready-to-use condition, requiring no further aging or decanting. When you are trying to determine if a Port needs decanting, refer to this simple rule of thumb: The wine is ready to drink straight out of the bottle if it is closed with a twist-out cork stopper that has a black grip top. If the bottle is closed with a regular cork, then the wine will probably require decanting.

Vinho Verde

In complete contrast to the richness and fullness of Port wines, Vinho Verde wines offer lightness and freshness as reflected in the name— Vinho Verde means "green wine." That description is indicative of a slight imma- turity or greenness that was once derived from a peculiar method of growing the vines. A simple shortage of

Vines being trained up tree trunks.

available farmland led the local population to resort to planting vines next to existing trees and training the vines up the trunk and onto the first bough of the trees. Because of this, the grapes were shielded from excessive sunlight by the trees' foliage and cooled by the breezes blowing through the valley. Thus the grapes rarely reached full maturity.

Although those growing practices have been all but abandoned,

DECANTING WINE

Although the need to decant a wine is rare, it is useful to know why and how to do it. There are two good reasons to decant a wine. The first is to separate the wine from the tannic sediment that has been deposited in the bottle during storage in a cellar. The sediment is composed of tannin that has fallen out of suspension in the wine. By separating the wine from the sediment, the wine remains clear, and the astringent tannins will be left behind in the bottle.

A second reason is to vigorously aerate a young wine that is not showing its full aroma or flavor characteristics. The action of streaming the wine from the bottle into a broad-based decanter pushes air into the wine and encourages the release of esters, chemicals that provide the sensations of smell and flavor.

The steps in decanting are as follows:

1. If the wine is an old bottle with a deposit of sediment, it is preferable to stand the bottle upright for a day or two prior to decanting so that the sediment falls to the bottom of the bottle.
2. If you have not stood the bottle upright in advance, you may want to take it from its horizontal position in the cellar and place it in a decanting basket.
3. Remove the foil capsule and the cork. If the bottle has been standing upright, you can do this with the bottle standing on a flat surface. If you are using a decanting basket, the cork should be removed while the bottle is in the basket.
4. Hold the empty decanter firmly in one hand, or have it positioned upright on a flat surface. Hold the bottle (in the basket if necessary) in the other hand, about one third of the way up from the base of the bottle.

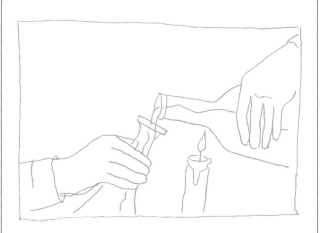

5. Begin to slowly pour the wine from the bottle into the decanter with the shoulder of the bottle positioned over a source of light. In a restaurant, the source of light would usually be a candle. At home you can use a flashlight. The light is there so that you can look down through the shoulder of the bottle and see the wine flowing out of the bottle with the light shining behind the wine. You may want to have a funnel in the neck of the decanter. For restaurant use there are fancy silver funnels, but at home plastic works just as well.

6. Continue to pour steadily and slowly until you see a streak of hazy material moving into the shoulder of the bottle. If the wine is in a Bordeaux shape bottle with the exaggerated shoulder, this haze will collect there.

7. If you see significant hazy material or solid bits moving into the neck of the bottle, stop pouring by gently raising the neck of the bottle.

There will usually be about half an inch to one inch of wine left in the bottom of the bottle. You should accept that this small quantity of wine is lost.

Box continued from previous page

the style of the wine has not changed. In fact Vinho Verde is produced as red, rosé, and white, although it is only the white that makes it to the export market. The typical Vinho Verde displays high, fresh acidity, green fruit characteristics, and a slight "spritz" or effervescence on the tongue. The best grape varieties for Vinho Verde are Alvarinho and Loureiro. If the wine is made from 100 percent of either variety, the grape name will appear on the label.

Germany

There really is no reason to ignore or avoid German wines. They offer everything that the modern consumer wants in wine—diversity, quality, purity of flavor—and they partner excellently with many foods. However, like all things, wine is fashionable, and German wines have been out of favor for a while, principally because

everybody believes they are all sweet and white, and the wine fashion police tell us that we should be asking for dry white wines or reds.

In my opinion, the biggest favor wine drinkers can do for themselves is to expand their horizons and that means exploring wines of all nations, including Germany. Not only does Germany offer excellent examples of dry whites, but in the next decade we will see an increasing number of reds as well.

German wines have their own classification system that is approximately equal to the appellation systems of France and Italy, although the basic premise is somewhat different. The following label terminology will help you decipher German labels.

Label Terminology

Older German wine labels have been rightfully criticized for being too cluttered and intimidating, but a closer look at current labels shows that the modern German wine maker is aiming for something simpler and more direct.

Like all labels on quality wine, German labels provide information about the region and the producer. The principal regions represented on the export market are Mosel-Saar-Ruwer, Rheingau, Rheinhessen, and Pfalz.

Almost all German wine labels give the name of the grape variety, the most famous one being Riesling. In addition to place and grape, there are a few other words that provide hints about the style of the wine, especially with respect to dryness, quality, and intensity of flavor.

DRYNESS LEVELS

A dry German wine will be indicated by the word *Trocken*: not surprisingly, *Halbtrocken* suggests half-dry, or off-dry.

QUALITY AND FLAVOR INTENSITY

The term *Qualitätswein* is used for wines from any one of Germany's official regions made from authorized grapes that have reached the required level of maturity, as measured by the sugar content of the juice after the grapes have been pressed or crushed. All this means is that the grapes were ripe, and there is every reason to believe that the wine will be good.

The German classification system then goes on to the *Qualitätswein mit Prädikat* level. This level of the classification has six subcategories. If the term *Qualitätswein mit Prädikat*, or QmP, shows up on the label, it immediately means that there will be an extra term (one of the six subcategories) that gives an indication of how ripe

This old-fashioned label shows the wine is a Qualitätswein mit Prädikat, and that the grapes were picked at Spätlese ripeness level.

the grapes were at harvest, as measured by sugar levels, and how intense the flavors will be. The six subcategories are

- Kabinett—normally ripe grapes, more intense flavor than just *Qualitätswein*; could be dry or a little bit sweet; if dry, the word *Trocken* will probably be on the label;

- Spätlese—a little more intense flavors than Kabinett; could still be dry; if so, the word *Trocken* will probably be on the label;

- Auslese—more intense flavors still; most Auslese wines are noticeably sweet; again, the presence of the word *Trocken* or *Halbtrocken* will indicate a dry or half-dry wine;

- Beerenauslese—this undoubtedly indicates a sweet wine, with Botrytis characteristics;

- Trockenbeerenauslese—a very sweet, Botrytis-affected wine, with very intense flavors;

- Eiswein—very intense flavors and very high sweetness levels from grapes that were allowed to freeze on the vine.

The German government recently authorized the inclusion of an additional quality-related term on German wine labels. First, a little background. Critics of the above terms complain that those words are only about how much sugar was in the grapes at harvest, and that such terms do not recognize that certain vineyard plots are more capable than others of producing quality wines. Those critics have argued for decades that the name of specific vineyards is a far better gauge of quality than the level of sugar at harvest.

In response, the German wine authorities have agreed to categorize some of the demonstrably superior vineyards in German regions as *Erstes Gewächs*, the equivalent of the French phrase *Premier Cru*, or First Growth.

So, producers of wine from single vineyards that have been recognized as *Erstes Gewächs* are more concerned about putting the name of the vineyard on the label than the exact *Prädikat* designation. For example, many quality-oriented producers are harvesting their grapes at *Prädikat Auslese* level, but not putting those words on the label. Instead, they identify the wine as *Qualitätswein*. Basically, they are afraid that consumers will assume that the word *Auslese* will be translated as sweet when it is not the case.

WINE NAMES

Although the way that German producers name their wines is in a state of flux at the moment, the following model is generally applicable. There are four levels of labeling: regional, village, producer blend, single vineyard.

Regional: If we start from the assumption that the grape variety name will appear on the label, the most basic form of labeling is by region. An example of regional labeling would be "Rheingau Riesling," indicating Riesling grapes from the Rheingau region.

Village: The next level of labeling would be village level, with the name of the village appearing on the label, such as "Rudesheim Riesling," or "Rudesheimer Riesling." The addition of the letters "er" at the end of a village name in German indicate that the wine is "from" that village, just like New Yorker, or Londoner. For the same reason, many German labels use "er" in conjunction with the vintage year, such as "2003er."

Producer Blend: Many high-quality producers have reached the conclusion that their name alone is a significant indicator of quality and that consumers will trust that judgment. I believe it is a well-founded belief. From that perspective, there is an increasing number of wines where the prominent pieces of information on the label are producer name and grape variety name. In practice, this is no different than the labeling habits of most producers in Australia or the United States. A typical example from Germany would be Bürklin-Wolf Estate Riesling. Most often, the region will also be identified on the front or back label.

Single Vineyard: For those producers who are fortunate enough to have access to grapes from a single vineyard, German wine regulations allow the name of that vineyard to appear on the label.

GEORG BREUER

Montosa
CHARTA

RHEINGAU RIESLING
1998

A more modern German label. This one is for Breuer's Estate Riesling, named Montosa. It is from the Rheingau region.

There are two formats for this. The traditional way is to label the wine with both the village name and the vineyard name. For example, the name Bernkasteler Doctor indicates that the wine was made from grapes grown in the Doctor vineyard, which is located in the village of Bernkastel. (Again, the addition of the letters "er" show that the wine is "from" the village of Bernkastel.)

A recent trend has been to downplay the village name and highlight the vineyard name. An example would be a wine labeled "Berg Schlossberg." This indicates that the wine was made from grapes grown in the vineyard called Berg Schlossberg. On the back label would be a notation showing that the Berg Schlossberg vineyard is in the village of Rudesheim, as well as a notation indicating that the village of Rudesheim is in the region of Rheingau.

Grapes

There is no doubt that Germany is Riesling country—Riesling at its best. But the wonderful thing about German Riesling is that it has a distinctive profile depending on which region it comes from. In recent years, the Riesling grape variety has reclaimed land that it had lost to higher yielding but lower quality varieties, and its return is very welcome.

In addition to Riesling, there are small quantities of Pinot Gris (Grauburgunder or Ruländer) and Pinot Blanc (Weissburgunder) planted, but the number two white grape in Germany is Muller-Thurgau, widely planted in Rheinhessen where it produces attractive but simple wines.

Despite the common belief that Germany only makes white wines, there are several red wines made there as well, and the number is growing rapidly. Traditional grape types have included the Portugieser and Trollinger, though they make rather commonplace wines. However, the red grape that has everybody's attention currently is Pinot Noir, and it shows great promise, although there is only a handful of good examples at the moment.

Regions

As mentioned earlier, Germany's principal wine-producing regions are Mosel-Saar-Ruwer, Rheingau, Rheinhessen, and Pfalz. Here is a more in-depth look.

MOSEL-SAAR-RUWER

This region is centered on the Mosel river as it meanders slowly northward on its journey to join the Rhine river. The Saar and Ruver are both small rivers that flow into the Mosel. It is very picturesque countryside, with many turns in the Mosel river that create broad but steep hillsides that have been transformed into

The steep hillside vineyards of the Mosel. The section in the foreground has been replanted with new vines.

a sea of vines clinging precariously to their respective slopes. This is Riesling territory, with most of the wines produced in what is referred to as the "classic" style, i.e., a distinctive note of sweetness along with high acidity, allowing the production of the world's classiest "sweet and sour" wine. Mosel wines (as they are usually referred to) are prized for their delicate nature and fine balance between the sweetness of fruit and the fresh acidity. They are traditionally marketed in tall, slim, green bottles, as opposed to the brown bottles of the other regions described below.

RHEINGAU

Monopolizing the north bank of the Rhine river as it flows from east to west for about twenty miles, the Rheingau vineyards are an impressive sight. The south-facing slope provides many prime locations where all of nature's bounty seems to have been brought together for the purpose of fine wine making.

It may be an exaggeration to say that the current dry white wine revolution started here, but there are certainly many important proponents of the trend in this region. They claim that the fashion for making German wines sweet was an aberration that began after the Second World War and reached its height in the 1970s and '80s with brands like Blue Nun. A number of prominent wine makers in this region are committed

Newly planted vines, protected by plastic sleeves, in the Rheingau region of Germany.

to returning to what they consider a more authentic dry style, rather than manipulating the wine making process to render the wine sweet. Again, the most important grape is Riesling. Compared to the wines of the Mosel, Rheingau Rieslings have earthier characteristics and a firmer structure to accompany the distinctive citrus fruit aromas and flavors.

RHEINHESSEN

Most of the Rheinhessen is an elevated plateau lodged between the Rhine river to the east and north and the Nahe river to the west. It lies directly to the south of Rheingau.

This region produces a large quantity of simple, attractive, slightly sweet, fruity wines from the Müller-Thurgau grape variety. Recent activity in the northeastern part of the region, where the vineyards slope down to the Rhine river, have concentrated more on Riesling made in a dry style.

PFALZ

Farther south of the Rheinhessen is the Pfalz region that stretches all the way to the border with France: Just across that border is Alsace, where French wine makers make many fine white wines. Protected by mountains to the west, the region enjoys many sunny days throughout the growing season, which is reflected in the fuller, riper flavors in the wines. Again,

Riesling is regaining ground in the vineyards, and a few quality-minded wine makers are promoting their single vineyard wines, or *Erstes Gewächs*, when the vintage conditions produce an excellent harvest.

Austria

Austria has recently become a highly regarded wine producer, particularly revered for its dry and sweet versions of Riesling. The nation also boasts its very own Grüner Veltliner grape, which makes very attractive, aromatic, and fruity white wines with just a suggestion of spiciness in the aroma. In addition to these two staples, there is a broad range of white and red grape varieties grown. Of those, the most likely candidates for the export market are Chardonnay (also known as Morillon in Austria), Pinot Blanc (Weissburgunder), Pinot Gris (Rulander), and even Cabernet Sauvignon.

Austria uses similar label terms as Germany to give the consumer an idea of the ripeness of the fruit at harvest and, therefore, the flavor intensity of the wines. The principal regions to look out for are Kamptal, Kremstal, Neusiedlersee, Thermenregion, and Wachau.

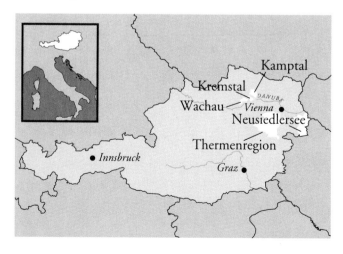

Chapter 3

IN THE
RESTAURANT

In the Restaurant

When a customer enters a restaurant with the intention of dining and choosing a wine, an immediate need arises. The customer wants and needs to know what is available to eat and drink. Food menus and wine lists have two major functions: to inform and to sell. All diners and service staff would do well to understand that the best designed menus and wine lists are

intended to perform those two functions. Some wine lists achieve that goal better than others.

Wine lists come in all shapes and sizes, from the formal leather bound volume, printed on fine paper, to the low-key chalkboard. Whatever the presentation of the wine list, the important thing is that you be able to navigate your way around it. That navigation will be easier if you understand the basic precepts of a wine list and the possible variations in format, content, organization, and pricing.

What the wine list looks like and what it contains should be a function of two major questions: What is the restaurant trying to be, and what does the restaurant want to provide to its customers? In other words, all restaurants can be categorized as having some kind of overriding theme that determines everything to do with style, quality, and price in the restaurant, and all restaurants have a pretty good idea of what their customers are looking for in terms of product and service.

It makes sense for an all-American restaurant to offer only American wines, since they obviously fit with the "theme." Similarly, Italian restaurants can reasonably restrict their wine selection to Italian wines. What management and the service staff have to determine is whether that narrow approach is acceptable to the clientele.

For example, the all-American restaurant might determine that

WHITE WINES

CALIFORNIA
Chardonnay, Cakebread, Napa Valley, 2002
Chardonnay, Lolonis, Mendocino, 2001
Chardonnay, Iron Horse, Sonoma, 2002
Sauvignon Blanc, Buena Vista, Sonoma, 2002
Fumé Blanc, Murphy Goode, Napa, 2001
Riesling, Trefethen, Napa, 2002
Gewürztraminer, Navarro, Napa, 2002
Viognier, RH Phillips, Dunnigan Hills, 2002

OREGON
Chardonnay, Domaine Drouhin, Willamette Valley, 2002
Chardonnay, Adelsheim, Willamette Valley, 2001
Pinot Gris, King Estate, 2002

WASHINGTON
Riesling, Hogue, Columbia Valley, 2002
Viognier, Cayuse, Walla Walla, 2002

This wine list is broken out by location.

the customer base is eager to try wines from many different parts of the world, and will therefore include wines from any one or more of the southern hemisphere nations that label wine by grape variety, just as the United States does. Or, the management team of the Italian restaurant could justifiably consider including wines made from Italian grape varieties (such as Sangiovese or Pinot Grigio) that are grown in other areas around the world.

The most interesting wine lists also give heavy consideration to the types of food offered in the restaurant. The question may be as simple as whether the restaurant is a steak house or a seafood restaurant. But there are other food and wine considerations that are best explored through reading the chapter on Food & Wine (pages 177-188). For example, mildly spiced dishes respond well to certain types of wine that should be available on the wine list, while sandwiches and burgers will call for a different approach. Regardless of cuisine and the dishes offered, all good restaurants should include at least one selection of a red, white, and rosé by the glass.

Ordering Wine

With the tremendous range of restaurants available to us now, it is no surprise that we like to eat out so much. And whether you're having a light lunch or a formal dinner, it is easy to master a few simple steps so that ordering wine is hassle-free. When you have done this a couple of times it will seem like second nature, and you will wonder what all the fuss was about.

How Many Glasses & Wines?

Wines by the glass mean you can pair a different wine with each course of a meal.

The first consideration is whether you want one glass of one wine, two or more glasses of the same wine, or two or more glasses of different wines. This is important because it will point you in a certain direction in looking at the wine list and ordering the wine.

If your intention is to use the same wine throughout the meal, then you will be looking at the bottle selections on the list. If you want only one glass of wine, or two or more glasses of different wines, then you will want to ask the waiter about the availability of wines by the glass, and check that section in the wine list.

Restaurants that are committed to providing the diner with quality and selection offer a large number of wines by the glass. The advantage of this to the consumer is that you can enjoy one glass of a lighter style of wine with an appetizer dish, and another glass of a fuller-flavored wine with your main course.

Getting the List

Ideally, the waiter will bring you the wine list automatically. However, that doesn't always happen, so you may have to ask for it. In some instances, asking for the wine list will be a good response to the question that all waiters seem to ask: "Can I get you something to drink?" The waiter has been told to ask that question because drinks are a profit center for most restaurants. If all you want is wine, now is the time to make it known.

While you have the waiter's attention, take the time to ask if there are any specials, or if there is a wine-by-the-glass section. If you are still a little uncertain about making a selection, you might ask if the waiter has any suggestions or recommendations. In addition, you might inform the waiter that you prefer wine with lots of ripe fruit, or that you don't like too much wood in wine, or that you are looking for

A light white wine is an excellent aperitif.

something with high acidity. The waiter's response will give you a good idea of how much he or she knows about the list and the wines on it.

If you choose to have a drink of wine or something else before dinner, you usually do not need to worry about what food you intend to order. Most people choose their before-dinner drinks for pleasure. If you want your aperitif to perform a function, go for something that is light and simple, with high acidity, as this will cleanse the palate and help to stimulate your appetite. In this regard, a simple sparkling wine is an excellent choice.

Wine List Organization

All wine lists are organized in one way or another, but the extent of categorization will depend upon the number and variety of the listings. Better wine lists are user friendly and easy to negotiate, encouraging diners to find a wine that they are willing to buy. Having said that, consider that the selection of a wine from any list is made easier if the customer can easily determine the color of the wine, the grape variety, and/or the geographic origin of the wine. Each specific wine listing should also include the exact name of the wine (grape variety, geographic place name, or proprietary brand name), producer name, any appellation information, and vintage date.

The most frequently used wine list categories are wine style, grape type, and geographic area. The categorization system will depend on how many nations and which nations are represented on the wine list, as well as on the number of wines included. Better restaurants will also have a clearly identifiable selection of wines by the glass.

Wines Listed by Wine Style

This system works well for short lists. The basic approach is to list wines under the headings of Sparkling Wine, White Wine, Rosé Wine, and Red Wine. Any wine listed under each heading would then need to indicate wine name, producer, region of origin, and vintage date. (This system can work equally well for wines from one country or from several countries, as long as the nation is identified in each individual listing.)

Wines Listed by Geographic Area

This system is quite flexible. It could easily be applied to a wine list that has only American wines, or wines from the United States, Australia, and New Zealand. Whether the system is applied to Europe or the United States or anywhere else, the restaurant must decide what the extent of the geographic breakdown will be. Will it be by nation only? Or will the wines be broken down by state? And, within each state, will they be broken down into individual appellations? The most common versions group the wine listings by nation under the broader headings of color. If the wine list has numerous entries, the national groupings would then be broken down by state or region.

Wines Listed by Grape Type

Grape type headings are very common in restaurants around the world, because of the increasing number of wines that are labeled by grape variety. The system lends itself well to incorporation in a list that also uses wine style categories, so that there could be a major heading of "White Wines" with the wines then broken down by grape variety heading such as "Chardonnay," "Sauvignon Blanc," and so on.

This format makes it easy to find your favorite wine type, and also gives you a good opportunity to look for something unusual or that you've never tried before. However, it has major limitations when it is applied to European nations, since many European nations use place name as the name of the wine. It is also difficult to use with wines made from two or more grape varieties (which is a common practice in many wine making regions). With blended wines, the restaurant therefore has to decide whether it is comfortable using headings such as "Cabernet-Merlot," or "Cabernet-Shiraz," which you may see on menus using this format.

Pinot Noir

Acacia, 2001, Carneros, CA

Robert Sinskey, 2000, Napa Valley, CA

Sanford, 2001, Santa Barbara, CA

Calera, Mills Vineyard, 2000, Mt. Harlan, CA

Ponzi Reserve, 2000, Willamette Valley, OR

Knudsen Erath, 2001, Willamette Valley, OR

Millbrook, 2001, Hudson River, NY

Merlot

Clos du Bois, 2000, Sonoma, CA

Duckhorn, 2000, Napa Valley, CA

Jekel, 2001, Monterey, CA

Arbor Crest, 2000, Columbia Valley, WA

Waterbrook, 2001, Columbia Valley, WA

Bedell, 2000, North Fork of Long Island, NY

Cabernet Sauvignon

Mayacamas, 1999, Napa Valley, CA

Frog's Leap, 2000, Napa Valley, CA

Alexander Valley Vineyards, 2000,
Alexander Valley, Sonoma, CA

L'École #41, 2000, Walla Walla, WA

Chateau Ste.-Michelle, 2000, Columbia Valley, WA

Pellegrini, 2000, North Fork of Long Island, NY

A wine list organized by grape type.

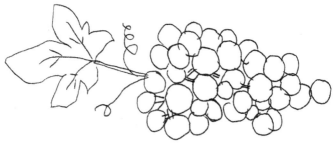

Wines by the Glass

Often restaurants advertise the wines that are available by the glass in a separate section that is subsequently broken down by color, and then possibly categorized by grape type or place. Alternately, wines by the glass will simply be identified within the body of the list, either by the use of a separate column for glass prices, or by some kind of icon (like a wine glass) placed next to the bottle price. For restaurants that offer more than one wine of any type (color, or grape type) by the glass, a higher-priced and lower-priced selection will often be available.

A well-organized wine list is a helpful tool for customer and wine waiter alike. As long as the customer has a basic understanding of what types of wine he or she likes, the customer or waiter can then quickly scan the list for wines from the appropriate grape type and climate.

Wines by the Glass

WHITES
Chardonnay, Iron Horse, Sonoma CA   6.50
Chardonnay, Adelsheim, Willamette Valley, OR   8.50
Sauvignon Blanc, Buena Vista, Sonoma CA   5.00
Pinot Gris, King Estate, OR   5.00
Viognier, RH Phillips, Dunnigan Hills, CA   5.00

REDS
Pinot Noir, Sanford, Santa Barbara, CA   6.50
Pinot Noir, Knudsen Erath, Willamette Valley, OR   8.50
Merlot, Clos du Bois, Sonoma, CA   6.00
Merlot, Arbor Crest, Columbia Valley, WA   8.00
Cabernet Sauvignon, Alexander Valley, Sonoma, CA   6.00
Cabernet Sauvignon, L'École #41, Walla Walla, WA   8.00

Wines listed by the glass.

Pricing

A wine list in a casual restaurant.

If you are anything like the average restaurant patron, you probably think that most wines in restaurants are overpriced. And I would have to agree with you, but there are exceptions. All I can do here is give you some idea of how most restaurant managers approach the pricing of wines and then suggest ways in which more perceptive managers and owners view pricing strategies.

The standard approach of most restaurants is to mark up all wines by two-and-a-half to three times the wholesale cost. While this is understandable and acceptable for lower-cost wines, it doesn't make sense for more expensive wines. That is to say, if a wine costs the restaurant $7.00, I can see why they might put it on the list at $20.00. The restaurant needs to make a profit of $13.00 from that sale in order to cover all of the ancillary costs involved in serving that wine. But, if a wine costs the restaurant $70.00, I don't see why they need to charge $200.00 for it. It doesn't cost $130.00 to serve the wine!

So, better restaurants use a sliding scale or a set dollar mark-up system for more expensive wines, based on the knowledge that, with aggressively priced wines at the higher-cost end, they will sell more of those wines and make a higher profit by selling more bottles at a lower price. Following this logic, the bottle that costs the restaurant $70.00 might be priced on the list at $120.00, or even $100.00, giving the restaurant a profit of $30.00 or $50.00 on the sale. And my contention is that the restaurant will sell many more bottles at $100.00 or $120.00 than it will at $200.00.

Make Your Selection

One of the easiest ways to get through the wine selection process is to say to somebody else at the table, "I would really like it if you chose a wine for us!" However, if the task is to be yours, there are two initial considerations: Does the choice of food matter, and can you figure out how the list is organized?

If you are looking for a wine and food pairing that will work you should familiarize yourself with the concepts and information starting on page 177.

Choosing wine to go with food for one person is not hard, but dining alone is not recommended! Choosing wine for two diners is fairly straightforward. But tables of four and more make it very difficult to order one wine because of the wide variety of flavors that could end up on the table.

There are three immediate solutions to this dilemma: (*1*) encourage everybody to order their choice of wine by the glass, or suggest a glass of wine for them to try; (*2*) order two half bottles or two bottles of different wines (a full-flavored white and a full-flavored red, or a light-bodied red and a full-bodied red); (*3*) order a bottle of wine from a grape variety that is versatile with many different foods, such as Pinot Noir, Sauvignon Blanc, or Sangiovese.

When you have figured out how the list is organized, it should be relatively easy to go to the section that includes the wine you want. If you know you want Californian Merlot or Australian Shiraz, for example, they shouldn't be hard to find. If you're in the mood for French White Burgundy, and the restaurant offers it, you'll spot it easily.

If you want something unusual, then look around for the Viognier section in American white wines, or wines from southern Italy, or South Africa. It seems to me that restaurant dining is the time to experiment with wine and to develop new likes (and maybe a few dislikes!).

When you have made your selection, you need to communicate that to the waiter. If the wine list uses a number system for each wine, it is okay to ask for the wine by number. It is also okay to point. In fact, it is even a good idea to point so that you know the waiter has understood what your selection is.

Check the Bottle

The waiter should bring the unopened bottle to the table. If all is going well, he or she will present the bottle to you with the label visible for you to check that it is the wine you ordered. Even better, the waiter may announce what the wine is. You should be checking that the name of the wine, the producer, the region, and the vintage are the same as you ordered from the wine list.

What do you do if any of that information is different from the listing? You should tell the waiter so that he will (hopefully) take steps to make sure that the listing is updated. In the modern wine market, it is unlikely that any change in information would be so dramatic that you would want to change your selection. It would require an in-depth knowledge of the market to predict any variation in quality based on a change of vintage (though the vintage charts at the end of this book might be of interest in this regard).

Assuming you are satisfied with the bottle brought to the table, you should indicate to the waiter that he may open the bottle.

Check the Cork

Right up front I want to tell you that I have given up checking the cork. I have seen too many corks to want to look at another one. I am not interested in touching the cork—they tend to be slimy and sticky. And the last thing I want to do is smell the darn thing. There seems to be a general notion that smelling the cork will tell you if the wine is bad. Well, here's the big secret: cork smells of . . . cork! In my opinion, the only way to find a bad wine is to check the wine, not the cork.

However, you may disagree. So here are the steps: (*1*) Check the cork visually to see if it is excessively dry or slimy; and (*2*) smell the cork to see if there are any dank, cellar smells.

If either of these conditions exists, you may have a bad wine, but you should still proceed to the smelling/tasting stage that comes next.

By the way, while the waiter is opening the bottle, the best thing you can do is ignore him. Don't stare. Just assume that he knows what to do. And if the waiter breaks the cork, you don't have to do anything—that is his problem! (See page 171 for more on this.)

Check the Wine

Assuming that the waiter opens the bottle success-fully, he will pour you a small portion to "taste." How much do you have to do? You need to do some-thing because the waiter is waiting for permission from you to pour the wine to everybody else at the table. But, this stage of the proceedings can be done very simply. Over the past several years, I have reduced my involvement in this stage to simply smelling the wine. If the wine smells clean, I tell the waiter to pour to the other guests. If the wine smells bad, I don't want to drink it, and I suggest you adopt a similar philoso-phy. Nobody should drink anything for pleasure if it smells bad. (See Good Wines Gone Bad, page 160, to determine the smell of "bad wine.")

GOOD WINES
GONE BAD

You may feel uncomfortable declaring a wine's no good if you don't know what to look for. The standard approach to tasting a wine (looking, smelling, tasting) should help provide clues that a wine is out of condition.

VISUAL CLUES

The principal visual clue is that the wine has a cloudy or hazy appearance. Such problems are very rare these days since technology provides wine makers with the ability to ensure that wines are completely free of foreign matter before bottling. However, it can happen, and if it does, the wine should be rejected.

Occasionally, white and red wines may have small crystalline deposits, visible on the cork when it is extracted, or in the glass as the bottle is emptied of wine. While you may think that this deposit is unsightly, it is not an indication that the wine is in bad condition. It simply means that the wine has been subjected to low temperatures since it was bottled, and the cold temperature has caused a small but insignificant amount of the acid content of the wine to precipitate and form crystals. This is not a negative factor and is not a good reason to refuse a bottle.

AROMA AND TASTE CLUES

There are four main problems that can sometimes be identified by smell and taste, even by a relatively inexperienced taster. Those problems are corked wine, hydrogen sulphide, volatile acidity, and oxidation.

Corkiness: To say a wine is "corked" means that it has been tainted by a bad cork. This happens when the cork itself is infected by a form of bacteria that subsequently turns the wine bad, as evidenced by the smell and taste of the wine. The scent is best described as that of wet, rotting cardboard in a damp basement. It has a dank ugliness to it. If you taste the wine, you will find that most if not all of its fruit character has disappeared, leaving an empty, hollow impression of what the wine might have been. Whether you recognize this fault by aroma or taste, the wine should be rejected.

Hydrogen Sulphide: This smell in wine is usually the result of an undesirable reaction between decomposing yeast cells and the sulphur that was added to prevent oxidation and bacterial spoilage. The identifying feature of this problem is a distinct rotten egg smell. In modern wine making, it is rare, but if you come across it, do not hesitate to reject the wine.

Volatile Acidity: To varying degrees, all wines have levels of volatile acidity— acids and acetates that are natural components of the fermented wine. However, high levels of volatile acidity give the wine a harsh, vinegary smell, and the fruit component on the palate is likely to be masked. If you find a vinegary smell is too unpleasant, ask for the bottle to be replaced.

Oxidation: Oxidized smells occur in all wines as they age. Early stages of oxidation may be identified simply as a tired, flat, or dull aroma, with a lack of attractive fruit character. This stage of oxidation is often noticeable on wines served by the glass, when the bottle has been left open overnight or longer. In such circumstances you should not hesitate to ask for a new glass to be poured from a fresh bottle.

In white wines, more severe oxidation will result in a rancid or Sherry smell. Whereas Sherry and a few other wines like Madeira are meant to smell like that, the average Chardonnay and Sauvignon Blanc are not. Standard varietal white wines that smell like Sherry should be replaced. With red wines, an oxidized aroma will be similar to the smell of Port.

On occasion, if I am perplexed by the smell of a wine, I will taste it just to get a second opinion about the soundness of the wine. Whether you smell only, or taste as well is up to you, but you should let the waiter know if the wine is acceptable and if he can pour to your fellow diners.

Relax and Enjoy!

Hopefully all of your hard "work" will be worth it, and you will indeed enjoy your selection. If the waiter does not return to your table to refill an empty wine glass, it is okay to repour for yourself or your guests, though this should not be necessary in a high-end restaurant where you are paying as much for service as anything else.

By the way, if you order a second bottle of the same wine, the waiter should offer you the opportunity to taste the second bottle, and may offer you a clean glass to do so. Certainly, a clean glass is desirable. If you order a second bottle of a different wine, you should taste it, from a clean glass, and you should let the waiter know if you want all diners at your table to be given a clean glass. Good restaurants will do that automatically.

Serving Savvy

The act of opening and serving wine in a restaurant setting may appear to fall only within the domain of the waiter, but as the section on Ordering Wine (page 150) demonstrates, the customer is a crucial factor in the whole process, and a thorough knowledge of that process on the part of both parties is likely to ensure success. There are a number of useful hints in this section that will help anybody open bottles of wine with as few problems as possible.

Assuming that the task of ordering a bottle of wine from the list has been accomplished, then the remaining tasks of the waiter are to (*1*) make sure all the necessary equipment is in place;

(2) present the bottle to the customer to gain approval to open the bottle; (3) remove some of the foil covering the top of the bottle; (4) remove the cork from the bottle; (5) pour a taste portion for the customer; and (6) serve the other guests.

Equipment

The standard tools needed to open and serve wine include some kind of wine opener, glasses, and possibly some kind of vessel in which to keep the wine chilled.

WINE OPENERS

There are two basic types of wine opener, the standard waiter's corkscrew, and the cork puller. My own preference is for the corkscrew, but I do know many waiters who are very adept with the cork puller.

KNIFE
FOOT
SCREW

The functioning parts of the corkscrew are the knife (to cut through any foil), the spiral screw (to insert in the cork), and the foot, which allows the handle to be used as a lever to extract the cork.

The cork puller has two flexible prongs, one of which is longer than the other, to be inserted between the cork and the bottle neck, and an oval shaped handle or grip used to pull the cork out.

GLASSES

Many high-end restaurants have placed a lot of emphasis recently on the style and quality of wine glasses used. Does the shape and quality of the glass make a difference? I am afraid that the answer is a resounding YES! Simply put, anything will taste bad out of a diner mug. Fine porcelain and fine crystal allow the pure flavors of wine (or coffee or tea, for that matter) to be more easily appreciated, and how the shape of the glass is engineered will influence how the wine releases its esters (organic compounds that give wines their fruitiness), aromas, and flavors.

However, the simple practical consideration is that most

restaurants cannot afford a wide range of different glasses, particularly if they contain a high crystal content that makes them more likely to break! Once again, the theme of the restaurant, the quality level, and price level are going to dictate what kinds of glasses are used.

The three basic possibilities are an all-purpose glass (used for all wines served in the establishment), a white wine glass with an exaggerated tulip shape, and a red wine glass with a defined balloon shape. Ideally, any wine glass will allow for a serving of between four to six ounces, filling the glass only one third or one half full, with sufficient room left for the wine's aromas to be released but "captured" in the bowl of the glass.

In addition to those basics, there may be a need for a sparkling wine glass that will be either a very narrow tulip "flute" shape, or a more exaggerated "trumpet." Although the champagne saucer might still be used for banquets and weddings, it went out of fashion a long time ago in restaurants, as it tends to dissipate the bubbles more quickly.

CHAMPAGNE FLUTE

CHAMPAGNE TRUMPET

WINE CHILLERS

Certain types of wine seem to taste better when they are served chilled, and in order to maintain their flavor profile it helps if those wines are maintained at a lower temperature during service. The standard approach has always been that white wines, rosé wines, and sparkling wines are served chilled, while red wines are served at room temperature. Following those guidelines will usually bring acceptable results, but it may not be the best approach.

A desirable serving temperature for wines is a function of the wine's fullness of body and intensity of flavor. Regardless of color, full-bodied and full-flavored wines taste better at warmer temperatures, while light, delicate wines taste better chilled. Based on that premise, a light-bodied Gamay or simple Chianti (both red wines) might be better served colder than a barrel-fermented Chardonnay. To appreciate this model, try drinking a room temperature Budweiser and an ice-cold Guinness, and see if either one of them tastes good!

WINE SERVICE TEMPERATURES

- *60ºF/15ºC*   Full-bodied red wines
- *55ºF/12.8ºC*   Light-bodied red wines and full-bodied white wines
- *50ºF/10ºC*   Medium-bodied white wines
- *45ºF/7.2ºC*   Light-bodied white wines, rosé wines, and sparkling wines

The point here is that a waiter might recommend that a white wine not be kept chilled, or that a red wine be served chilled. By the same token, customers might request that their wine be chilled or not.

In addition to the general premise that all sparkling wines and all rosés should be chilled, determining the relative weight of the wine (review Wines by Grape Type on pages 26-39 for more on this), might give you grounds for experimenting with different serving temperatures for different wines.

Assuming that the restaurant keeps some wines in a chilled condition ready for service, the basic options for keeping the wine cold during service are an ice bucket or a wine chiller. Let me say right up front that ice buckets are clumsy, and they get in the way. They can work, but they require lots of attention. The preferred contents of the ice bucket are two parts ice to one part water, with enough volume (about half full) to have a chilling effect on the wine in the bottle, but not so much that everything overflows when the bottle is put into the bucket. The ice bucket should be placed on a stand next to the table, but tucked out of the pathway of waiters and other customers.

An ice bucket should be two parts ice to one part water.

Also, the bottle needs to be wiped or protected with a napkin to prevent dripping cold water onto customers or the table.

The wine chiller is a simple cylindrical ceramic or stone container that is refrigerated before use and maintains its cool temperature for long enough during service to keep the wine chilled. It is convenient (it can be placed directly on the table), easy to use, and requires much less labor and clean-up.

The label should face the customer when the bottle is presented.

Presenting the Bottle

When the waiter brings the bottle to the table, he or she will present it to the customer who ordered the wine. This is the customer's opportunity to confirm that the wine brought to the table is the wine ordered. The easiest way for the waiter to do this is to cradle the bottle on one arm with the base of the bottle resting in the palm of the hand. With the label clearly visible to the customer, the waiter should announce the name of the wine, and then wait for the customer to agree that it is the correct wine.

Having received permission to open the bottle, the waiter may step back slightly from the table, but should not leave the table. By the same token, it is better if the diners now leave the waiter to do his job, rather than pay any attention to the opening of the bottle.

Removing the Foil

Most bottles of wine still have some kind of foil sleeve over the top, and a portion of this has to be removed so that the cork is exposed. If you are using a corkscrew, open up the knife blade and use it to cut through the foil around the neck of the bottle, approximately one-half inch from the top of the bottle. Most bottles have a ridge around the neck at this point, making it easy to place the knife blade under that ridge, and then run the knife blade around the neck. If you use a cork puller, this action can be done with the sharp edge of one of the prongs.

When you have cut through the foil, use the knife blade (or prong on the cork puller) to pull up the edge of the cut foil so that you remove the top portion of the foil. (If you are a waiter, the foil should be placed in your pocket.)

Some wine makers have dispensed with the neck foil on the bottle, opting instead for a paper or plastic disc on the top of the cork. Obviously this means you can bypass the foil cutting step, and go straight to inserting the corkscrew or cork puller.

Removing the Cork

First of all, you need to figure out where you are going to execute this task. If you are using an ice bucket, you should keep the bottle in the ice bucket and extract the cork there. If you are using a wine chiller or no chiller at all, then you can use a corner of the table if there is room, or a side table if it is directly next to the customer's table. Some people object to waiters who open wine bottles in the air. Personally, I see nothing wrong with it, and in many cases, a lack of space in the restaurant may dictate that this method is used. In any event, this step should be done within the immediate scope of vision of the customer. You cannot retire to the bar or to kitchen to open the bottle.

Using a corkscrew to get the cork out of a bottle is not that hard if you use the principles of physics upon which the corkscrew is based. It's all about leverage. First, you need to get the corkscrew into the cork, and the key here is to get the corkscrew down through the center of the cork, and deep enough

The point of the corkscrew should be placed just off center.

so that you can pull the entire cork out of the bottle.

Bear in mind that the center of the corkscrew is not its point. The center is the hole down the middle of the spiral; the point of the corkscrew is slightly off-center. So, place the point of the corkscrew slightly away from the center of the cork, push the point in, then turn the corkscrew in a clockwise direction to drive it down through the cork. You should continue turning the corkscrew down through the cork until the final half of the spiral is left showing above the cork.

Now, position the "foot" of the corkscrew on the rim of the bottle, and hold the foot in place with a thumb or finger.

Wrap the fingers of your other hand around the handle of the corkscrew, and begin to pull straight upward on the end of the handle. It is important to pull straight up, and not in an arc—if you pull in an arc toward the bottle, you will break the cork, leaving a portion of the cork in the neck of the bottle.

You should now be in a position to grasp the cork between your thumb and forefinger (do not touch the lip of the bottle) and twist the cork out of the bottle. There is much debate here as to whether one should "pop" the cork or not. It seems to me that it depends on the wine and the environment. If you are serving a bottle of fine, expensive wine in an elegant, formal setting, I don't think it is appropriate to pull out the cork with a loud pop. But I see nothing wrong with doing that on a bottle of good, but ordinary, wine in a noisy café or bistro.

If you are using a cork puller, the steps are as follows: On one side of the cork, place the longer prong in the space between the cork and bottle and push it down a short distance. Then insert the other prong on the opposite side of the cork between the cork and bottle neck.

Once both prongs are inserted, rock the puller from side to side, pushing each prong down bit by bit on either side of the cork. When both prongs are fully inserted, grasp the handle and pull upward with a twisting motion. The prongs of the cork puller have a concave shape that allows them to grip and pull out the cork as you pull upward.

If you then remove the cork from the corkscrew or cork puller, you should follow the restaurant's policy as to what to do with the cork. I have already made it clear that I personally don't want to see it. But if it is house policy or the customer requests to see it, it should be placed on the table next to the customer's plate setting. Some restaurants insist on using a small plate or saucer to place the cork on.

Pour a Taste Portion

Regardless of what you do with the cork, you need to move onto the next step. Pour a small portion (about 1 ounce) of the wine for the diner to taste, and then wait for the customer's approval. You may have to prompt the customer to taste the wine ("Would you like to check the wine before I serve it to the guests?").

If a customer tastes the wine, and then says that the wine is not what he or she was expecting, or that there is a problem with the wine, it would be normal practice for most waiters to call a manager to the table to discuss the matter with the customer. If the restaurant has empowered the waitstaff to deal with such matters, so much the better. As already stated, it is my hope that the restaurant would accommodate the customer's wishes, regardless of whether the customer simply doesn't like the wine or there is something truly wrong with it.

Assuming that there are no problems and you are given permission to continue pouring, you should leave the taster's glass as is, and follow any restaurant policy as to what order or sequence to serve the other guests. Some restaurants like to serve all females first, other establishments simply suggest moving around the table in one direction, pouring to each diner as you go. Whatever

When pouring wine, be sure the bottle does not touch the glass.

the policy is, the last guest to have the glass poured should be the taster.

When pouring, it is best to stand to the right of the customer. In many restaurants it is impossible to do this, however—there simply isn't room. In such circumstances you may have to reach across a guest or across the table, but be sure to apologize for doing so.

Pour slowly to avoid spills and splashes. At the end of the pour, lift the neck of the bottle to stop the flow of wine, and then twist the bottle about one-eighth of a turn. This should make any drips run down the neck of the bottle, where they can be wiped with a napkin as you move on to the next customer.

As a waiter in a restaurant setting, you need to get used to recognizing how much is an appropriate pour from a bottle of wine. Most restaurants use a regular pour of five or six ounces. Since there are approximately twenty-five ounces in one wine bottle, you have to figure out how much you should pour in each glass to ensure that everybody gets about the same amount. It is normal practice to fill the glass only a third to one-half full, leaving room for the wine's aromas to collect in the bowl of the glass. At all costs, you must avoid not having enough for the final pour. This takes practice, and you may need to work on it on your own time, getting used to the different shapes and sizes of glass used, and getting to know how far you can stretch a bottle.

Remember as well that not everybody may want wine, so be alert to diners' spoken requests and body language. When you have served wine to everybody who wants it, you can place the bottle on the table, or in the bucket or chiller if there is still wine left in the bottle. If the bottle is empty, you might ask if the customers want the bottle left, or if you can take it away and bring a second bottle or another selection.

It should then be the ongoing job of the waiter to ensure that

WHAT TO DO IF YOU BREAK THE CORK

If you break the cork in two, leaving a portion of the cork in the bottle, the first thing to do is to figure out what went wrong so that you don't keep repeating the error. There are two probable causes of the breakage. Either the corkscrew was not driven far enough into the cork, so you were effectively pulling only half of the cork out. Or, you pulled the handle in an arc rather than straight up.

Now you have to deal with the problem. If this is all taking place in a restaurant, the waiter should address the problem at the table. Again, the customer can do nothing at this point but wait until the server has completed the task. When a cork breaks off and leaves a bit in the neck of the bottle, the break usually leaves an uneven surface on the remaining cork. Try to find an area on the cork's surface where you can gently push in the point of the corkscrew sideways. Slowly and gently turn the corkscrew in a clockwise direction to begin driving the screw down through the cork. You will have to be careful that you do not push the corkscrew through the bottom of the cork as this may dislodge a piece of cork into the wine in the bottle.

When you think you have secured the remaining portion of cork on the corkscrew, use the foot and lever system to bring the rest of the cork out of the bottle. If the restaurant policy is that the cork be placed on the table, the waiter should simply place both pieces on the table. Of course, it would be a good idea to express your apologies to the customer for having broken the cork.

By the way, the whole problem of broken corks can be avoided by using a cork puller. In addition, synthetic corks are far less likely to break, and screw caps never break!

the table's wine needs continue to be met. This means watching the diners' glasses to see if repours are necessary, though it is always a good idea to check with each customer to be sure he or she wants more wine. If the first bottle of wine has been finished, then you should ask if another bottle of the same wine is desired, or if a different selection from the list would be preferred.

If the same wine is requested, you should bring a clean tasting glass to the diner who is coordinating the wine choices. It is usually a good idea to make sure a glass is empty of wine from the first bottle before pouring wine from the second.

If the table orders a completely different wine, it would be appropriate to bring all new glasses for everybody.

The Cork vs. Other Closures

When I entered the wine industry twenty-five years ago, rumors abounded that there was a serious shortage of cork. Those rumors are still being spread today, but they may not matter in the slightest. There is a much more serious problem than availability if wine makers want to continue using cork stoppers, and that problem is suitability. Stated bluntly, wine is too fine a beverage to be stoppered with a piece of tree bark, particularly if that tree bark is susceptible to infection by bacteria that subsequently taints the wine in the bottle.

The debate over whether to continue using cork closures has been particularly fierce over the last ten years, with the development of synthetic corks and the promotion of screw caps as alternatives.

So, what is the problem with real cork? During the sterilization process in preparing cork, a latent bacteria in the bark seems to react with chlorine to form a chemical called trichloranisole, or TCA for short.

The annoying thing about the presence of TCA is that it is extremely hard to detect, it is completely random, and it will result in a tainted wine that smells like old, musty newspapers and has no fruit character at all.

The true extent of this problem is very hard to pin down, mostly because the vast majority of ordinary wine drinkers do not recognize the smell as being a fault, and blithely proceed to drink the wine under the mistaken impression that it is supposed to smell that bad! Proponents of alternative closures suggest that a full 10 percent of all wine bottles suffer from some degree of "corkiness." Defenders of real cork suggest it is closer to 1 percent. In my experience of having opened hundreds of bottles of wine for tasting and consumption, I would have to agree that the figure is closer to 10 percent.

The various camps have launched major public relations campaigns to present their cases in favor of real cork or other closures. In the meantime, there have been some identifiable trends.

SCREW CAPS

Major producers in Australia and New Zealand have surged ahead in the use of screw caps for many of their white wines, convinced that, of the closure choices, the screw cap is the most efficient and reliable. Those wines have been in the export markets for about two years now, where they seem to have been accepted, albeit somewhat reluctantly at first. The irony is that the person who would benefit most from the widespread adoption of the screw cap—the average wine drinker—is exactly the person who will resist it most, simply because the average wine drinker equates the screw cap with low quality.

Importers and distributors of wines with screw caps have been working closely with restaurant and retail outlets to educate waitstaff and consumers as to why screw caps are chosen. One immediate issue is what becomes of the opening ritual at the restaurant table. Well, as you might have realized elsewhere in this section, I have had serious concerns about that ritual for many years now. Maybe it is time for the wine industry and restaurants to step into the twenty-first century, and embrace the screw cap as a technology that protects the wine from spoilage. All that changes at the table is that the waiter and the customer do not have to deal with a cork. That sounds like a good development to me.

To emphasize their support of screw caps, a few pioneering producers of high-end ageable red wines have made the switch. One recent and remarkable example of this occurred when a highly respected producer of $150.00 Napa Valley Cabernet Sauvignon decided to seal half the bottles with cork and half with screw caps. To demonstrate its commitment to and belief in the screw cap, the producer charged $10.00 more for the screw cap bottles, arguing that the quality of the wine was guaranteed.

With the recent pronouncement by respected British wine author Hugh Johnson that he is in favor of screw caps for wines that will be consumed within two years of production, we are likely to see more and more producers moving in that direction.

SYNTHETIC CORKS

Synthetic corks represent something of a compromise in the closure argument, offering a hint of the "romance" of real cork, but avoiding the dangers of TCA taint.

A large number of producers, particularly in the United States and Australia, have chosen this option, and most of them seem very satisfied with the switch. A few early trials seemed to go astray with severe oxidation occurring very quickly in some wines, but the technology continues to advance and the synthetics seem to be getting better all the time. However, some producers have found that wines with synthetic corks take on a plastic taint if stored for more than two years. One major synthetic cork producer reacted to this by developing a model specifically designed for wines that will be aged. The producer claims that it has almost identical properties to real cork, without the potential for the "corked" taint.

The principal problem cited in connection with synthetics is that sometimes the corks are very difficult to extract, resulting in embarrassing moments for waitstaff who must struggle to serve their customers. Other considerations are that the corks are almost impossible to reinsert, and they are not biodegradable (though they can be recycled).

Wine corks are made from the bark of the cork oak tree.

REAL CORKS

The argument to keep this traditional closure is based mostly on romance and custom. When a cork is in good condition, there is no doubt that it can be an excellent stopper for wine. After all, cork is a remarkable natural product. It can be squeezed small enough to insert into a bottle's neck and expands naturally to grip the inside.

But problems arise not only with bad corks but with good corks as well. By their very nature, no two corks can be identical. Each one has a unique pattern of cells, and therefore will behave differently. It is probably this difference that accounts for what wine enthusiasts call bottle variation: the tendency for two bottles of the same wine to show variations in taste, flavor, and aroma, even though they were purchased at the same time, and stored in the same conditions. As exciting as bottle variation might sound, I think that most wine lovers would prefer consistency in the same wine from the same vintage.

Undoubtedly, the ritual of removing the cork from a bottle to serve a customer has more elegance than twisting off a screw cap. And the final outcome of all this may well be that more expensive wines will continue to be stoppered with cork, while simpler, everyday versions will adopt an alternative. If that happens, the cork industry may implement more quality checkpoints in the production process in an attempt to reduce the number of TCA-tainted corks. A win-win situation!

Chapter 4

FOOD
&
WINE

Some wines can be intriguing and beguiling by themselves. Certain foods seem complete and fulfilling. But there is something extraordinarily felicitous about the interaction and symbiotic nature of food and wine that makes most pairings greater than the sum of their parts. With food and wine, there are marriages that seem made in heaven, marriages that work, and marriages that will always seem contentious.

In more than a quarter century of talking to wine makers, I have noticed one constant thread: Producers want to make wines that people enjoy. They want to make wines that are part of the dining experience, when human interaction reaches new heights over the simple convention of eating. And, in many parts of the world, it is visibly true that most consumers view the table, especially the dinner table, as the primary opportunity to enjoy wine.

So, what can be done to ensure that the combination of food and wine is the best that it can be? In what ways may these pairings be made more rewarding? I believe that there are some simple techniques any person can use to construct a complementary menu that makes the food and the wine taste better individually and, even better together. One has only to apply some basic principles that relate to the tastes, flavors, and textures of any pairing.

To understand these principles, let's look first at the traditional approach to food and wine, and then consider some alternatives that could further enhance the dining experience.

Traditional Approach

We have all heard that white wine goes with fish and white meat, and that red wine goes with red meat. This is undeniably true. It works. And in many ways, this approach is very useful. Its functionality lies in the fact that it recognizes the role of color. Some will see this as a simplistic method, but I promise you that it works.

But more important than the colors of the meat are the colors of the vegetables. I have suggested elsewhere in this book that the aromas and flavors of wine can be thought of as having fruit characteristics, but specifically the characteristics of green, yellow, red, or black fruit. If you have any one of those fruit components or suggestions on the plate, then it makes sense to echo those components with the same kinds of flavors in the wine. Following this theory, a green vegetable aroma in a cool climate Sauvignon Blanc would be well matched with fresh asparagus or green beans, and the earthy, red fruit component of Merlot might be echoed in the use of red beets on the plate.

Such associations are particularly useful when there are different color versions of the same fruit. For example, just as there are green tomatoes, yellow tomatoes, and red tomatoes, it is a reasonable assumption that differently colored wines would go with each. The green tomatoes might go best with a cool climate Sauvignon Blanc or Riesling, whereas yellow tomatoes would pair better with Chardonnay or Viognier, and red tomatoes would be well matched with a Gamay or Pinot Noir.

In other words, the colors of all the foods on a plate are important in a wine consideration, but it is the color of the vegetables in

The mineral flavor of Champagne nicely complements the briny, beachiness of raw oysters.

particular, rather than of the meat or fish, that play the most significant role. To wit: White wine can work very well with red meat, and red wine can work equally well with fish. So, what makes such combinations work?

Alternative Guiding Principles

Untraditional combinations of food and wine can be successful if thought is given to the intensity of the wine and food, and/or the function of the wine in the context of the meal.

Principle #1: Keep in mind that matched foods and wines should have approximately the same intensity of flavor and weight. It is easier for food and wine to achieve a harmonious working relationship when the basic ingredients of each are of equal strength. Conversely, imbalanced combinations never seem to work. For example, when a full-flavored, rich meal, like duck confit, is matched with a light, delicate wine like Beaujolais, or when a full-bodied Syrah is paired with a veal scaloppine, neither pair is particularly good.

Principle #2: Decide what function you want the wine to perform. Do you want the wine to enhance the food by providing similar flavors, tastes, or textures? Or do you want the wine to highlight the food by providing a counterpoint or contrast of flavors, tastes, or textures?

Intensity of Food and Wine

There are two issues that will affect the intensity of flavor of the food: the ingredient itself and the method of preparation. While it would be impossible to list all the possible foods and cooking methods of varying intensity here, the following should help give you a rough idea of where things fall on the flavor-saturation spectrum. Think of it as the periodic table of food!

FOOD & COOKING-METHOD
FLAVOR INTENSITIES
(Items are ordered from least intense to most intense)

Food	Cooking Method
Sole	Steam
Flounder	Poach
Scallop	Boil
Bass	Sauté
Cod	Grill/Broil
Shrimp	Roast
Trout	Braise/Stew
Chicken	
Halibut	
Veal	
Turkey	
Salmon	
Pork	
Swordfish	
Tuna	
Duck	
Beef (Tenderloin)	
Steak	
Venison	

When pairing wine with any food, it is important to think not only about what type of food you'll be eating, but also how it will be cooked. It is also crucial to be absolutely clear about what part of the food ingredient is being used, which in turn may drive the cooking method. For example, there is a big difference between a skinless duck breast and a whole duck. The whole duck would necessitate a more aggressive cooking method, such as roasting or braising, whereas the duck breast would respond much better to a sauté or grill method.

In addition, the intensity of flavors will be affected by any sauce that might accompany the main ingredient. Scallops with a simple citrus beurre blanc are a different matter from scallops with a red pepper coulis or a sauce based on a lobster reduction

The creamy richness of lobster bisque is well matched with a heavy, buttery Chardonnay.

and enriched with butter. The beurre blanc would work better with a light wine like a Chenin Blanc or Sauvignon Blanc, whereas the red pepper coulis would pair well with a medium-intensity Pinot Noir, and the lobster reduction would call for a heavier, richer Semillon or Chardonnay. Following is a table showing the variations in wine intensities. As with food, a wine's "strength" is determined by both the raw ingredients and methods used to make it. (Many producers provide information on the front or back label as to the wine making method used. Wines by Grape Type, on pages 26-39, will also give you a good idea of whether wood was part of a wine's aging process.)

WINE AND METHOD FLAVOR INTENSITIES

Wine

Riesling (White)

Pinot Grigio (White)

Chenin Blanc (White)

Sauvignon Blanc (White)

Pinot Blanc (White)

Pinot Gris (White)

Gamay (Red)

Chardonnay (White)

Pinot Noir (Red)

Viognier (White)

Sangiovese (Red)

Marsanne (White)

Cabernet Franc (Red)

Merlot (Red)

Tempranillo (Red)

Zinfandel (Red)

Cabernet Sauvignon (Red)

Syrah (Red)

Method

- 100 percent stainless-steel fermentation
- 100 percent stainless-steel fermentation, plus 100 percent short wood aging or 50 percent of wine in wood for longer
- 100 percent stainless-steel fermentation, plus 100 percent long wood aging
- 100 percent barrel fermentation and aging

From this consideration of intensities, we can conclude that a lighter, more delicate wine such as a stainless-steel–fermentation Riesling or Pinot Grigio would be a good accompaniment to poached seafood, whereas a wood-aged Chardonnay or Pinot Noir would be well matched with sautéed or grilled salmon or pork, and barrel-fermented Syrah would pair well with venison in a rich red wine reduction.

Function of the Wine

When considering the function of the wine in a meal, the principal question is whether to use similarities to enhance the food and wine, or contrasts to highlight them.

ENHANCING WITH SIMILARITIES

The desired result here is to match a flavor, taste, or texture in the food with a similar flavor, taste, or texture in the wine. Familiarity with the flavors of different wines comes with practice, and, again, the descriptions in Wines by Grape Type on pages 26-39 are a useful guide. As a consumer, you can always inform the waiter or

The intensity of a barrel-fermented Syrah is on par with that of hearty venison.

store clerk that you are considering a particular dish, and that you are looking for a wine with certain flavors to enhance the experience. Good waiters should take the time and effort to develop a memory bank of what kinds of flavors can be found in the wines on the restaurant list. Again, there are many permutations, but following are some suggestions that will help you to develop your own ideas:

Matching Flavors:

- Apple flavors in Chardonnay with apple accompaniment for pork
- Spice flavors in Gewurztraminer with spice-rubbed pork loin
- Black pepper flavors in Syrah with black pepper in the dish
- Nuttiness in Chenin Blanc with sautéed trout with almonds
- Earthiness in Pinot Noir with mushrooms
- Smokiness in wood-aged Merlot with grilled meats

Matching Tastes: One rule of thumb is to pair acidic wine with acidic food. There is a general feeling that wine does not go well with salad. This is true if the salad dressing is heavily influenced by the acetic acid of straight vinegar. However, if you use natural citrus juices, like lemon, or flavored or sweet vinegars, such as raspberry or balsamic, then wine can work very well with salad. A high-acid wine such as Albarino from Spain or Gavi from Italy will appear to cancel or reduce the overall acidic effect, leaving the natural flavors of both the salad and wine to shine through. It's a bit like the mathematical phenomenon where a negative times a negative equals a positive!

Crisp Sauvignon Blanc and tangy goat cheese are delicious together.

This "acid x acid" method doesn't only work with salad. For example, pairing a high-acid wine like Sauvignon Blanc with a high-acid goat cheese can be delicious. This blissful match is best illustrated by the pairing of Sancerre from the Loire Valley in France, and a chèvre from the same region, though similar results can be achieved by using Sauvignon Blanc from other cool climates, like New Zealand, or parts of South Africa, and pairing them with goat cheese from anywhere.

And of course, there is the rule that puts sweet-tasting wine with sweet food. Here, the tastes do not cancel each other out, per se. Rather, when sweet wine is paired with dessert, the wine should always be sweeter than the food. Thus, late harvest and botrytis-affected wines become excellent partners with fruit-based desserts such as fruit tartlets, pies, or poached fruits. The sweeter wine serves to bring out the natural sweetness of the fruit.

Textures: The two possibilities here are combining a smooth wine with a smooth, rich, or creamy food, or combining a sharp, crisp wine with a sharp, crisp food. The decision to match textures will depend, of course, on the individual, but it may also depend on the season. (For example, the pairing of a buttery seafood dish with a similarly rich wine may seem comforting in winter, but might be overly heavy in the warm summer months.)

The similar textures of lobster with butter and a buttery Chardonnay make them an ideal match.

When determining the richness of a food, keep in mind that cooking methods like braising or stewing provide a deep, silky mouthfeel, especially if the food ingredient is high in natural fat or gelatinous matter. Alternatively, regardless of cooking method, thick, buttery, creamy, or heavily reduced sauces can provide richness. Since you will be attempting to echo that texture in the wine, the key is to find a wine with a rich, smooth mouthfeel that therefore enhances the richness of the food. For example, a lobster with butter might work well with a rich, buttery Chardonnay. Or duck confit, preserved in its own fat, might be well matched with a smooth Grenache Syrah Mourvèdre blend from Australia, or from the Rhône Valley in France.

The combination of crisp wines and sharp foods is usually associated with pairing tart, tangy foods and bright, light wines, such as ceviche with Vinho Verde from Portugal, where both the food and the wine have an angular edge that enhances the experience. High-acid wine, such as Barbera from Piedmont in Italy, served with a high-acid cheese, like Asiago, is another example of this.

HIGHLIGHTING WITH CONTRASTS

This approach is, frankly, more common, and may even ensure a greater degree of success. Highlighting with contrasts is a method that has been favored for decades by chefs who provide different foods on the same plate in order to exhibit different tastes and textures. Based on that premise, it is easy to simply consider the wine as an extension of the ingredients, and to treat it the same way, i.e., with the potential to provide contrasts of taste or texture (flavor, alas, does not really figure in here).

The pungent saltiness of prosciutto is offset by the slight sweetness of Gewürztraminer.

Contrasting Tastes: The collective group of salty or cured items, especially meats and fish, find a beautiful complement in wines with prominent fresh fruit character and even slight sweetness. The pairing highlights the flavor of the wine and of the food itself, so that the salty component is less noticeable. Examples of this combination include fruity Gamay or Pinot Noir with smoked or cured meats, like ham or turkey, and fish, such as trout or salmon. A similar result is achieved when a fruity or noticeably sweet wine is paired with blue or other salty cheeses.

When dealing with a light amount of natural sweetness in foods such as scallops or lobster, it can be a good idea to counter that taste with a highly acidic wine that will, in effect, wipe the mouth clean and avoid a build up of the sweetness, so that every mouthful of the food continues to exhibit its fresh, attractive character anew.

However, a word of warning in dealing with sweetness on the plate: Sometimes chefs are tempted to "enhance" fruit sauces by adding sugar. The assumption that a dry (i.e., not sweet) wine will be a good contrast to that sugariness is a mistake. Sweetened sauces on the plate tend to mask the inherent fruit character of any dry wine. It is a better tactic to try to find a wine with a small amount of residual sugar, such as a Chenin Blanc, or maybe a Pinot Gris from Alsace, which will somehow "manage" or tame the sweetness in the sauce and allow you to enjoy the natural fruit flavors of the sauce and wine.

With sour or vinegary foods, such as pickled herring, the lightly sweet fruitiness of a wine like Moscato from Italy or California is a refreshing treat, highlighting the flavors of both the food and the wine.

The other possible taste element in food is bitter, and it may seem a natural conclusion to reach for a wine with some sweetness, but this may not be the better solution. Try instead an acidic wine with foods that have just a light touch of bitterness, and you will find that the acidity is capable of eliminating much of the bitter taste, allowing you to enjoy the natural flavors of the food. If you need confirmation of this theory, reflect on the fact that salad greens (which have a natural bitterness) have for years been served with acidic dressings, precisely because the acidity counteracts the bitterness.

Contrasting Textures: It is unlikely that you would be successful in contrasting a sharp or crisp texture in food with a rich, smooth wine since the flavor intensity of the wine would probably be too great for the food. But, contrasting rich, smooth foods with rough or sharp wines is another matter. Richness in foods can come from fat, butter, cream, and gelatinous substances, or even from the natural smoothness of things like pasta or potatoes. The contrasting possibilities for wines with such foods would be either sharp, high acidity, or rough tannins.

For example, the high acidity and accompanying angular feel to a cool climate Pinot Noir would be a good counterpoint to the fatty decadence of salmon. By the same token, the usually dense texture of lobster flesh, especially when dipped in butter, would be well-contrasted by a simple Muscadet from the Loire Valley in France. Note that earlier, the lobster dish was used in an example of pairing richness with richness, using a buttery Chardonnay to enhance the buttery lobster. These two examples are illustrative of the fact that trying to learn a long list of perfect matches is a waste of time. Preferences will change from individual to individual, from place to place, season to season, and even from dining partner to dining partner. Knowing your options is a much more interesting approach.

As for the smooth food contrasted by rough tannins, the combination here really affects the wine more than the food. In this case, it is the food that rounds out the tannins, masking their rough astringency so that the full flavors of the food and the wine can be enjoyed. The biggest problem that tannic wines present for the diner is the drying effect tannins have on the mouth—in the absence of saliva, it is impossible to taste or savor much of anything. But by using rich, meaty foods to smooth the tannins in rough red wines, the full impact of both the wine and food can be more readily appreciated. So, that big, aggressive, even surly Cabernet Sauvignon can suddenly become soft and luscious in the company of beef carbonade or prime rib. (Nota bene: Serving tannic wines with creamy sauces is a no-no. See What Not to Do, below.)

What Not to Do

There are a few combinations that will guarantee grim results just about every time, and I would encourage you to avoid them at all costs. First, foods that have a high salt content are rendered even more saline with high-alcohol wines, so when eating heavily salted foods choose a low-alcohol, preferably fruity, maybe even sweet wine. An ideal candidate would be a light- to medium-sweet Riesling from one of the German regions.

And, whereas it might seem rational to put a tannic red wine with a cream sauce or with fish, the result is usually awful—the disastrous duo creates an undesirable metallic reaction in the mouth. Low-tannin reds or full-bodied whites would be a safer choice.

Whether you are serving wine or enjoying it yourself, you will find that the application of these simple principles will result in a more satisfactory experience for everybody.

Chapter 5

FROM THE
STORE BACK
TO YOUR
PLACE

Buying Bottles

Today's wine enthusiast lives in a blessed world: Never before has there been so much wine available, nor so many different types. As delightful a situation as this is, it brings with it the daunting problem of picking your way through myriad selections in the hope of finding something that will suit your palate and bring you pleasure. Apart from buying wine in restaurants, there are several retail options available to the modern wine consumer. These include wine stores, winery tasting rooms, wine clubs, and the Internet.

Wine Stores

The experience of buying wine from a retail store can vary depending on where you live. This is because national and state or provincial governments have different laws about who can sell

The expansive wine section in a large supermarket.

wine and even what kinds of wine can be sold in certain stores. Nations like Sweden and Singapore reserve the sale of all alcoholic beverages to a government monopoly, so that wine is available only in government-run stores. The same is true of certain states in America and provinces in Canada. Most other nations and a number of states in the U.S. allow wine to be sold in large supermarkets along with other food items and in small "mom and pop" corner grocery stores. Given the variety of outlets, the act of shopping for and buying wine can be different from place to place, but the guidelines for making a successful purchase are generally the same.

WHAT IS THE WINE FOR?

Before you go to any store, it helps to know the purpose of your purchase. Are you buying for a special dinner, casual drinking, or with a view to storing the wine for long-term aging? If your aim is one of the first two, the wine will probably be for immediate use, or consumed within the next few months. The romantic notion that people have well-stocked cellars is pretty much a thing of the past, unless they are serious and wealthy collectors of wine. Most people do not have the room or the time to maintain a cellar full of wine that will suit their every need, so the vast majority of all wine sales are intended for consumption fairly soon after purchase. I once saw a statistic claiming that at least 80 percent of all bottles sold in the U.S. are consumed within forty-eight hours of purchase—that is probably a conservative estimate.

If your intention is to drink the wine within a day or two or even within two months, then you need to feel satisfied that whatever wine you choose is ready for consumption. Here again, things have changed. Only a very small portion of wine produced today is intended for aging. Wine makers know that people do not have wine cellars, and that they buy wine when they need it, so wine must be ready to drink. In this regard, it is only the sturdiest reds, such as Cabernet Sauvignons, Amarone from Veneto, and Syrahs from specific vineyard sites, which are not generally ready for drinking when bottled. That leaves the field pretty much wide open for finding a red, white, or rosé wine that is drinkable when purchased.

The category of wine for casual drinking is full of pleasurable bargains. Everyday house wine needs to be simple, but enjoyable. It is not necessarily about complexity, or soil, or out-of-body experiences. And it should not be expensive. Buying wines from nations as diverse as Argentina, Australia, France, and Italy, I have managed to keep my cost of basic house wine at a maximum of $8.00 per bottle. Keep in mind, however, that I live in the U.S., where there is a fairly competitive wine market that keeps the price of such wines within the reach of most consumers. If you live in a "controlled" state or nation where the government closely regulates the distribution and sale of alcohol, the price is likely to be closer to $12.00 for the same bottle.

In regions with a competitive wine market, decent bottles can be quite inexpensive.

Many of these casual, everyday wines carry a brand name such as Yellow Tail or Gossamer Bay. These brands offer well-crafted wines that represent solid value, with clean, fruity varietal characteristics. Their producers' basic philosophy is to offer consistent style and a reliable flavor profile to the consumer.

With wines for special occasions, you might want to be more adventurous and seek out wines with an individualistic character derived from a specific vineyard location or a certain wine making technique. No single nation holds the monopoly on wines for either casual drinking or special occasions—you can find what you are looking for from just about any nation.

WHAT KIND OF WINE DO YOU WANT?

Once you know whether you want something extra special or for everyday, you need to decide what style of wine you are looking for and how much you are willing to pay for it. If you have the time and a basic grasp of the fundamental information offered in the first parts of this book, it can be interesting, and even fun, to wander around the shelves of a wine store. You will also find it educational, as you see labels that remind you of something you have read about or perhaps tasted before. I have a very clear recollection of the early days of my first retail wine job in the wine department at Harrod's in London. The manager gave me a feather duster and told me to dust all of the bottles over in one corner of the department. When I had finished doing that, he directed me to another area of the wine shelves and told me to clean those bottles. And so it went for the rest of that day and through the next. I had begun to think that I would be dusting bottles for the rest of my life and that I should quit. On the third day, the manager said he thought I was ready to operate a cash register. And when my first customer asked for a wine from a specific village in Bordeaux, I knew exactly where on the shelves I would find it. For a couple of days, I hated that manager, but he knew what he was doing.

Most of the information you need to select a wine is on its label. And remember that back labels can be a gold mine of information. You should be looking for grape variety names that you know you like. With some European wines, that information may not be on the front label, but it might be on a back label. Or you may want to carry this book with you so you can refer to the information presented in Translating Place Name to Varietal Name on pages 42-57.

The wealth of information on the back label of this Napa Cabernet is similar to that you'd find on European back labels.

In addition to grape variety, you can get useful information from any statement of geographic origin on the label, particularly if you can relate that location to a warm or cold climate, which in turn will give you a good indication of the acidity level of the wine and its texture, whether it is smooth with abundant ripe fruit, or palate-cleansing with zingy acidity.

The other major piece of information on the label is the producer's name, but the usefulness of that comes only with experience. Over time, you will get to know which producers you like and think you can trust and which producers you feel you should avoid.

Many wine stores offer additional information about the wines, such as tasting notes or numeric ratings of the wine, and the usual source of this information is a wine periodical such as *Wine Spectator*, or *Decanter*, or Robert Parker's *Wine Advocate*. As useful as this information may seem, I think it has its drawbacks. Just because a wine is rated 95 points by a magazine does not mean that you are going to like it. If that were true, you would enjoy every movie that gets "two thumbs up." Whenever a consumer uses a reviewer's scores as a basis for purchasing or not, the consumer really needs to know what the reviewer's preferences are. In other words, scores are not much use without a full description of what the reviewer said about the wine. In fact, Robert Parker has threatened to sue stores that use his numeric scores without providing the written description of the wine.

Taking that criticism further, I would suggest that consumers are far better off shopping at stores that do not rely on third-party reviews of the wines, but that conduct their own tasting of every wine and provide their own assessments. In that way, a customer can easily get to know how his or her taste preferences align with those of the store operators and can even discuss the wine with the people who work in the store. In fact, the number one factor in making wine purchases easy for customers is the presence of a knowledgeable and helpful staff who diligently monitor all of the products they offer for sale. Building a relationship with that kind of store and the people who work there can be enormously rewarding in the long run.

HAVE A MIND OF YOUR OWN?

If you have the time and the will to browse through a store yourself, then you will need to figure out how it is organized. Given the enormous variety of wine available, it is just about impossible to organize a wine store in such a way that everybody will find what they are looking for immediately. Just as with wine lists, there are the basic choices of whether to organize solely by color, or by nation, or by grape type. But there will always be exceptions, and compromises have to be made. From my perspective, stores that sell CDs have the same problem. I rarely find what I am looking for immediately, until I figure out what the various categories are.

However, from experience, I can suggest that most stores start with a categorization by nation and then break the nation down into other areas such as states or regional appellations. This is especially true with European nations; for example, all of the Burgundy wines might be grouped together within the French section, or all of the Tuscan wines might be in one section of the Italian grouping. The alternative would be to group by nation, and then subdivide into grape types, with all of the Merlots together, all of the Chardonnays together, and so on. This approach is more likely with those nations that label wines by grape type.

The wines in this store are organized geographically.

In addition to the traditional methods of organizing a wine store, there are more innovative approaches that cater to customers' shopping strategies. Some stores have been particularly successful in placing a maximum price on the majority of all their wines, and organizing by wine style, with frivolous and humorous categories such as "Robust and Bold Reds," or "Kid-glove Whites." This can be particularly useful for those customers who know what kinds of wine they like, but are not married to a particular grape type or geographic area. It fact, it can result in some exciting experimentation and new discoveries of what else out there is enjoyable.

NEED HELP?

For those who are more pressed for time, the best thing is to ask for help immediately. This is where a store's investment in training knowledgeable and friendly staff who are familiar with the store's product line will really pay off, both for the store and the customer. But, as in the restaurant setting, the customer has to provide vital information that the store clerk can act on. From retail experience, I can assure you that store clerks have a million stories about customers' odd requests. ("I bought a red wine here last month; do you still have that one?" "I had a white wine last week that had a bunch of grapes on the label. . .") But by the same token, good store workers don't expect all customers to know everything about wine—so don't be afraid to appear unknowledgeable. Think of it this way: Very few of us understand the inner workings of our car, but that doesn't mean we don't talk to the mechanic when we get our car serviced.

The kinds of information that the store clerk can act on are your preferred grape types, levels of dryness or sweetness, degrees of tannin, extent of oak aging, soft and smooth textures, or sharp and mouth-watering acidity. Most important, don't be shy about specifying a price range. It is vital that the store assistant knows what you want to spend before he can think of products to suggest.

Depending on your geographic location, you may find that some stores promote wines through occasional in-store tastings. This is a good way for customers to try new wines and to capitalize on a reduced promotional price. In addition, if you can stand one more piece of mail or e-mail, sign up for the store's mailing list to receive catalogs or notices of special offers. You will find that there are often some good bargains at certain times of year, and you may even receive preferred customer status. One of the easiest ways to get preferential treatment is to buy wine by the case (twelve 750 ml bottles), since most stores will offer a discount of up to 15 percent on a case, even one containing a combination of wines.

Tasting Rooms

Most wineries around the world operate tasting rooms. These facilities not only provide stimulus to the tourism industry, they also represent a fun way to sample and purchase wine at the source. However, this does not necessarily mean that the wines will be less expensive, since the wineries do not want to be seen competing with the retail industry. Also, bear in mind that providing taste portions to an endless stream of tourists can get expensive, so be prepared to pay some kind of tasting fee. As a general guideline, be selective with what you taste. If your intention is to buy, then your primary consideration should be what you intend to use the wine for—casual drinking, a special occasion, or cellaring. You also need to have a clear head, so make sure that you spit during the tasting session. I know too many people who have ended up with a case of not-so-great wine that was purchased in the excitement (and haziness) of the moment.

A tasting at a winery in Burgundy.

By tasting specific varieties or styles of wine, you may indeed find that there is something you wish to purchase, especially if there is a generous case discount, which can be as high as 20 percent at tasting rooms. However, there is one potentially major snag: In some nations, it is illegal to buy wine in one state and transport it to another. This is certainly the case in the United States, where the Twenty-first Amendment to the Constitution gives the right to control the sale of alcoholic beverages to the individual states. Some states, though not all, insist that any alcohol brought into the state pass through the hands of a licensed wholesaler. To be absolutely sure about your legal status, you should inquire about the relevant laws where you live.

The same limitations may apply to purchasing wine at a winery in one state and asking them to ship the wine to your home state. In many instances, you and the winery may be breaking the law. In the U.S., there have been a number of legal challenges to this system, and things are changing so that there are now several "reciprocal" states that legally permit the shipment of wine from one state to the other. In addition, other states allow limited shipping with a permit, and a few more offer a "regulatory allowance." Currently, twenty-eight American states forbid any form of direct wine shipment into those states. For updated information on the status of shipping from state to state, you can access the Web site of the Wine Institute at www.wineinstitute.org.

In any nation where there is a state monopoly of alcoholic beverage sales, such as Norway and Sweden, there will be restrictions on shipping wines into that nation, and all shipments will be required to go through the hands of the national or regional monopoly. In other nations, shipping wine into the country or within the country is possible, but there are always limitations on the quantity that can be imported to an individual, and there may be customs duties and taxes payable. To be sure, you should check all local laws before attempting to ship wine.

Wine Clubs

One of the easiest ways to explore and discover new wines is to join a wine club that buys wines in large quantities at relatively cheap prices and distributes them to its members. Such clubs have faced lawsuits in regions that restrict the shipping of wines, so you should check the legal situation in your area. Assuming a wine club is legal, it is a great way to order wines from the comfort of your own home and have them delivered to your door. As with any mail-order purchase, the most important issue is whether you can trust the promotional sales pitch that accompanies the wine you're interested in. Since you are probably considering such purchases at home, you do have the luxury of being able to research the wine, its appellation, and its producer. Books, of course, are a great reference source, as is the Internet (for more on Internet shopping, see the facing page).

One of the joys of purchasing through a wine club is the possibility of finding something unusual, or available only in limited quantity, or hard-to-find wines from small wineries with no distribution system. Although wine clubs mean that the wine is being purchased in large quantities and should result in a lower price, bear in mind that there will be administrative overheads built into the cost of the wine, so that there may not be any appreciable savings compared to a similar wine purchased in a store. However, the convenience of this system can be very attractive.

Internet Sales

All of the warnings about legal problems related to shipping wine obviously apply to Internet sales. In addition, legal challenges have been raised regarding the question of sales tax. But assuming that there are no legal problems, using the Internet to buy wine offers all of the convenience of wine clubs with an even broader range of products to choose from.

There are numerous Web sites that promote direct shipment wine sales, including www.wine.com and www.buywineonline.co.uk. You can always look for online sites through any Internet search engine, and the Web site www.winespectator.com offers some very useful insights into buying strategies and selecting wines. Most of us find that there are certain producers whose wines we admire, and many wineries have their own Web site that may include information on how to purchase their wines online, or will provide a link to a wine club. If you find that the combination of product cost and shipping charges are too high, you can always combine forces with a friend or two to split the costs.

Drink Now or Savor Later?

There are three principal reasons to want to keep wine: short-term preservation after opening a bottle, short-term storage of unopened bottles, and long-term aging in the bottle. Different strategies need to be considered depending on your goal.

Short-term Preservation

Many people feel that they cannot consume a full bottle of wine in one sitting and therefore want to keep the unused wine for another occasion. While this is possible, you should bear in mind that all wines begin to change once they have been opened. A wine's exposure to air increases its rate of oxidation, which means that the natural fresh fruit characteristics in the wine will begin to fade.

If you slow down the rate of oxidation, however, you can keep an opened bottle of wine at least overnight and possibly up to forty-eight hours with only minimal changes. The easiest way to do this is to re-stopper the bottle and place it in the refrigerator. This is more difficult to do with synthetic corks (because they are hard to get back into the bottle), and easiest to do with screw caps, which create an airtight seal. Refrigeration can be used on all wines, but red wines should be removed from the fridge ahead of time so they can reach a warmer temperature for consumption. Despite re-stoppering and refrigeration, however, there will still be an appreciable amount of air in the bottle that will cause the wine to oxidize, albeit at a slower pace.

A more effective approach is to displace the air that is in the bottle. This can be done with a vacuum device that you attach to the bottle to pump air out. There are several versions of this apparatus available on the market, and they all work well. Many years ago, before the invention of such devices, some of my colleagues kept a quantity of glass marbles or beads on hand that they poured into the bottle to push the air out. The same effect can be achieved by planning ahead and, just after opening a full bottle of wine, pouring half of it into an empty, clean half-bottle, as close to the rim as possible. Once the half-bottle is stoppered, you can store it in the fridge or your usual storage area while you consume the wine remaining in the opened full bottle. You can find half-bottles (375 ml or 12 oz), and even twist-off cork stoppers at wine- and beer-making stores. I regularly keep six half-bottles available and have found that I can store a refilled half-bottle for at least a week, if not ten days, with minimal changes to the wine's aromas and flavors.

Of course, all of this would not be necessary if we could all buy the wine of our choice in half-bottle sizes in the first place. However, most producers do not offer that option since they have found that the costs of production are relatively high, and sales of that size tend to be slow. There are some producers who do provide half-bottles, and if you often consume less than a full bottle in a single sitting it might be worth your while to seek out a retailer who is willing to carry them.

Short-term Storage

If you adopt the habit of buying wine by the case to have bottles on hand over a period of weeks, then you should determine where you are going to hold those bottles and how. The main consideration is temperature and the need to avoid extremes. What we might feel is a comfortable ambient temperature for daily living can cause

This compact box can store more bottles than it seems.

changes in a wine. For example, very warm storage temperatures will cause a wine's fresh, bright fruit characteristics to fade and the wine to taste cooked. Such changes can occur quite quickly, so your principal concern is to find an area where the temperature will not exceed 65°F/18°C. You should also be sure to keep the wine away from sources of heat such as radiators, boilers, furnaces, sunny windows, and even the top of the refrigerator.

A small wooden wine rack that can be purchased from a home furniture store will suit most people's needs. If you are concerned about temperature, and if you have the money, there are a number of climate-controlled wine storage units that hold the bottles at a constant temperature.

Long-term Aging

The first things to understand about aging wine are that only a small percentage of all wines are made to be aged, and that old wine does not necessarily mean better wine. If you have never purchased wine for aging, but are interested in doing so, then you will probably want to get some expert advice. For a wine to age successfully, a few basic components need to be in place.

A good level of acidity is essential for a wine to age well, since it keeps the wine tasting fresh and alive, even at an advanced age. I can still remember the excitement at tasting, in 1983, a sweet white Loire Valley wine that was made in 1933. At fifty years old, the wine was still vibrant and energetic because of its elevated acidity level.

Alcohol and tannin can also help in the successful aging of a wine because both are natural preservatives. Still, they are not essential. Recently, I tasted a wonderful 1983 Riesling from the Mosel region of Germany that had no tannins and only 7.5 percent alcohol.

The key element to proper aging is a strong core flavor that is derived from the grape variety and sometimes enhanced by skillful wine making. Without that depth of flavor, an aged wine will simply taste hollow and uninteresting.

So, what kinds of wines age well? The most likely candidates are fuller-bodied reds, such as Cabernet Sauvignon, Syrah, Bordeaux blends, Rhône blends, Super Tuscans, and vintage port. However, the field is not restricted to reds. A number of cool climate whites with high acidity can also age extremely well. These include Chardonnay, Riesling, and Semillon, as well as most botrytis-affected white wines.

This wine cellar is ideal—quiet, cool, and damp.

But just because you age a wine does not mean that you will be impressed by the result. Old wine tastes different than young wine, but you may not find that you like it better. Fresh fruit fades to old, decomposing dried fruit in old wine, and some people distinctly prefer the grip and assertiveness of young, vibrant flavors. Perhaps the best approach is to accept that really fine, high-quality wines taste good at any stage of their lives, and the act of aging a wine simply means that you get to taste it at a later stage of development, witnessing its evolution from brash youth to suave senior. To get the most out of cellaring wine, you need to buy a minimum of six bottles of the same wine, preferably twelve, so that you can enjoy the wine on many different occasions and reflect on how it changes over time. The very worst that can happen is that you will get to the last bottle and it will be "perfect."

Long-term cellaring does require certain conditions for success. Simply put, you need a consistently cool, fairly humid place. The ideal climatic situation is 55°F/13°C with a humidity of 75 percent, which is often found in houses with a below-ground basement. But, more important than the actual temperature is the stability of that temperature—it should be as close to constant as possible. Extreme variations of temperature seem to affect the chemical composition of wine and change its flavor profile. It would be acceptable to have a gradual change from 60°F/16°C in summer to 50°F/10°C in winter, but if you have a daily temperature swing in that range, you need to take steps to control the climate.

Many serious collectors build expensive climate-controlled rooms that maintain a constant temperature, but you may also find that a small investment in a dehumidifier for the summer will serve the double purpose of cooling the air temperature and keeping the humidity in check. It is important to avoid excess humidity because it allows for the development of mold, which can eat through corks and damage labels.

If you don't have a basement or other cool, humid location, you can invest in a small cooler. These climate-controlled units, similar in size to a small fridge, are now widely available due to

Wine racks are ideal for long-term storage, since bottles can be placed on their side.

the increased interest in wine worldwide. They offer various capacities, some as low as forty-eight bottles, which makes them suitable for the occasional collector. Units such as these can be purchased in home furnishing stores, large discount stores, or restaurant supply outlets. Sub Zero is one of the leading manufacturers of wine storage units, and their Web site at www.subzero.com provides information on where they can be purchased.

The standard wisdom about cellaring wine is that the bottles need to be stored on their side. This keeps the wine in contact with the cork, and thereby prevents the cork from drying out and contracting, which in turn prevents the wine from seeping out and air from seeping in. Even if the entire wine world were to switch to screw caps, storing bottles on their side would still make sense—it is much more efficient than standing bottles upright. You will therefore need some kind of rack. This can be purchased, built, or adapted from the wooden wine case that some wines are shipped in. Even a simple heavy-duty metal shelf unit can be used to stack bottles on their side. Fully assembled, or in a DIY kit version, wine storage racks are also available from most discount stores or restaurant supply outlets, or you can browse the Internet for sites such as www.iwawine.com (International Wine Accessories), or www.wineenthusiast.com.

No matter if you are deeply serious about aging wine or not, having a space to store several bottles is desirable simply from the perspective that you will always have wine available for that unexpected occasion. Whether your purpose is to have wine on hand, or to perfect a wine through aging, maintaining a wine storage area can be a pleasure in itself—it makes you the proud owner of something that very few people have.

INDEX

Index